LIVE FAST DIE HOT

ALSO BY JENNY MOLLEN

I Like You Just the Way I Am

LIVE FAST
DIE HOT

JENNY MOLLEN

DOUBLEDAY

NEW YORK LONDON TORONTO SYDNEY AUCKLAND

All rights reserved. Published in the United States by
Doubleday, a division of Penguin Random House LLC, New York,
and distributed in Canada by Random House of Canada, a division
of Penguin Random House Limited, Toronto.

www.doubleday.com

DOUBLEDAY and the portrayal of an anchor with a dolphin are
registered trademarks of Penguin Random House LLC.

Portions of Chapter 1 originally appeared in *Cosmopolitan*,
"Sex & Relationships" (www.cosmopolitan.com), as "First Comes
Miscarriage, Then Comes Marriage" on January 7, 2014, and
"The Moment I Fell in Love with My Son" on March 12, 2014.

*Jacket photographs of Jenny Mollen and Teets © Deborah Feingold
Other jacket photographs: snow © matthaeus ritsch/Shutterstock;
mountains and foreground © Lizard/Shutterstock; fire © Tyler Panian/
Shutterstock; smoke © Asia Glab/Shutterstock; man © Chase Jarvis/
Stockbyte/Getty Images; planes © Pete Ryan/National Geographic/
Getty Images; sky © Hip Hip!/Alamy Stock Photo; fez © chrisbrignell/
Shutterstock; sled © trekandshoot/Shutterstock*

LIBRARY OF CONGRESS CATALOGING-IN-PUBLICATION DATA
Names: Mollen, Jenny, [date] author.
Title: Live fast die hot / Jenny Mollen.
Description: New York : Doubleday, 2016.
Identifiers: LCCN 2015045930 | ISBN 9780385540698 (hardcover) |
ISBN 9780385540704 (ebook)
Subjects: LCSH: Mollen, Jenny, 1979—Humor. | Actors—United
States—Biography. | Adulthood—Humor. | Conduct of life—
Humor. | BISAC: HUMOR / Form / Essays. | HUMOR / Topic /
Relationships. | HUMOR / Topic / Adult. Classification: LCC
PN2287.M655 A3 2016 | DDC 818/.602—DC23 LC record available
at http://lccn.loc.gov/2015045930

MANUFACTURED IN THE UNITED STATES OF AMERICA

1 3 5 7 9 10 8 6 4 2

First Edition

For Sid

CONTENTS

The stories you are about to read are basically true. Though I tried to do my best in depicting events as I remembered them, there are exaggerations, some characters are composites, some time periods are condensed, and some people's names have been changed to protect their anonymity. Except my mom's. Her name is Peggy.

INTRODUCTION

I never wanted to write a book about having a baby, mainly because I would never read a book about having a baby. After I saw the movie *For Keeps* with Molly Ringwald in 1988, I was pretty much scared off children for the next two decades. But when I hit thirty-four, my husband's biological clock started drinking and screaming at me before bed that it was time to put somebody else first. Him. So we got pregnant.

When Jason and I got married, I made all sorts of vows and promises, some of which I intended to keep (and others I just said in the moment to make him come faster). My life was exciting, sexy, and ever so slightly eccentric. I had a healthy relationship with a Hollywood actor who, despite my valiant efforts, remained more famous than me. He understood my neuroses, my fear of commitment, and my insistence on wearing his ex-girlfriend's beach caftan on vacation. He showed compassion when I got kicked off jury duty for accidentally befriending the defendant over lunch break. He even found it sweet when I invited our drug dealer to Passover seder because I didn't want him to think we were only using him for drugs. Life was fun, uncomplicated, and—aside from when our drug dealer found the Afikomen—predictable.

Then we had our son, Sid, and overnight, the fun-loving woman-child that my husband fell in love with was banished from our home. It was time to stop biting my nails, to stop bleeding through my tampons, to answer my cell phone, and to learn to do simple math in my head. But what if I didn't want any of those things? What if math hurt my feelings and super-plus tampons made my vagina feel fat? What if I wasn't ready to be a role model because I still envisioned being discovered at the mall and becoming a real model? (Or at the very least a Top Model.) Sure, I was thirty-five, but my boobs were only eighteen.

This book is as much about my reluctance to be a responsible adult as it is about my fear of vulnerability. The second Sid entered my life, all bets were off. I was in love like I'd never been in love, under the spell of a guy who would one day leave me for someone else. I felt terrified, unworthy, unprepared, and not at all hot. In an effort to outrun my own insecurities, my life turned into a cross between *Eat Pray Love* and *Die Hard*.

In retrospect, it probably would have been cheaper just to get back on Zoloft.

LIVE FAST DIE HOT

1

FIRST COMES MISCARRIAGE

How pregnant do I have to be before I can get an abortion?" I called out to Jason from the hotel bathroom, trying to sound rational.

I sat on the freezing-cold toilet, wearing only thermal socks and a headband, focusing intently on the plastic wand holding my destiny. Swallowing hard, ingesting one more moment of freedom, I tried not to look down at what I could already sense was a smug pink smiley face glaring up at me. Overwhelmed and unprepared, I fell into my lap, hyperventilating.

It was 2008, and Jason and I had been dating for only six months. Two months prior, we'd secretly gotten engaged in Saint Martin, but that was only because I'd found a picture of another girl's underwear on his phone and he didn't want me to jump to conclusions or light him on fire. I considered his proposal more of a negotiating tactic, a pillow-talk promise I could easily extract myself from if he turned out to be a philanderer or somebody who owned a bunch of aquariums. I was falling in love with him, but it was too new a feeling to trust completely. I'd never been in love and, I have to say, I didn't enjoy it. I was always more comfortable in relationships where I held all the cards, where I didn't have to feel and I couldn't get hurt—where there was always an easy exit.

Over Christmas I vaguely remembered taking ecstasy and letting Jason finish inside me, then washing down a morning-after pill with the next day's breakfast. I gave no thought to the notion that I could actually be pregnant. I wasn't even sure I *could* get pregnant. I was twenty-eight years old and I'd never been on birth control. At some point along the way I just decided that I was blessed. Accidental pregnancy was one of those things that happened to "other girls"—the ones in high school who smoked cigarettes and listened to Courtney Love.

Granted, I'd never let guys finish inside me. But it was the holidays, and I was feeling festive. It wasn't until a few weeks after New Year's that I suspected a problem. We were skiing with friends in Vermont when I started experiencing cramps that felt like I was being shived to death in a women's prison for not sharing my clarifying shampoo. My boobs were swollen torpedoes of estrogen. Every couple seconds I'd check behind me to make sure I wasn't turning my double black diamond red. I wasn't.

After two more days of waking up on unblemished sheets, I grew concerned and bought a pregnancy test. Like buying a Lotto ticket or a rolled-up drugstore scroll with my horoscope on it, I wasn't expecting more than a few seconds of entertainment, followed by a tinge of buyer's remorse.

Jason waited anxiously on the other side of the door as I hyperventilated.

"Well?"

"I can't breathe. This can't be happening. I'm gonna faint." I hobbled out of the bathroom and threw myself prostrate on the floor, hoping to instantly miscarry.

"Wow. Okay. Well, we can handle this." Jason picked me up and put me on the bed.

"I'm too young to be a parent, Jason. I'm a mere child myself." I thrashed around in a full-blown tantrum.

"You're twenty-eight. Actually, you're twenty-eight and a half, so basically you're twenty-nine," he said, thinking he was comforting me. "Let's take a beat and think this through."

"Okay . . . But I don't want a baby." I cloaked myself in a plaid comforter, assuming it made me invisible.

"Like ever?" He sounded concerned.

I'd pictured myself with children in the future, but before that I needed to be famous and have a booming acting career. The kind that would make my parents question why they hadn't paid more attention to me when they had the chance. I needed my ex-boyfriend to stop paying half my rent. And I needed my dad to stop paying the other half.

I had a life plan, things I needed to check off my list. If I was going to bring someone else into the world, I wanted to be able to take care of them, famously.

"Maybe someday," I said. "Just definitely not right now."

I spent the rest of the trip skiing like I was a stunt man in a Warren Miller film. I darted in and out of trees without braking, tried to complete an entire run on one leg, and even attempted a jump I'd researched on YouTube known as a "Screamin'

Semen." There wasn't any point in holding back; as far as I was concerned, life was over. I was knocked up, I was barely working, and I was only five months away from being twenty-nine, which was only twelve months away from being thirty, which was basically dead.

Three days later, I was still alive and Jason's screamin' semen was still burrowed inside me. We'd spent the last seventy-two hours (the same window, incidentally, that my bunk morning-after pill should have covered me for) weighing our options. Abortion was still tops on my list. Most of my girlfriends had survived them without complications or remorse. It was, after all, the twenty-first century. I was an independent woman living in a country that for the moment still granted me the freedom to make my own choices with my body.

The only thing holding me back was Jason. He wasn't some random dude I'd rear-ended while pulling out of the Rite Aid parking lot. Sure, I'd slept with that guy. But I obviously wouldn't have thought twice about aborting his baby. Jason was different. As much as I hated to admit it, he had a hold on me. And in my mind, having an abortion meant running the risk of ruining our relationship. I didn't want to look back and feel resentment toward him for allowing me to destroy something that was a part of us. Or have him hold it against me in fights. Like, "You forgot to put the cap back on the toothpaste, and oh, yeah, you killed our baby."

I wasn't ready to be a mother, and I sure as hell wasn't ready to start capping my toothpaste. I was living in a one-bedroom apartment with no furniture, and I'd thrown out all my dishes because I was too stressed out to wash them. But I was an educated adult woman, with money in the bank (that my dad and ex didn't know about) and a relationship that was actually making me feel something.

The more we talked, the more we realized we had to have the baby. The timing was a little off, yes, but we were in love, at least as in love as I was capable of being, and oh, yeah, we were secretly engaged already. We'd find a way to make it work.

When Jason broke the news to his mother, she was less than thrilled.

"You know, you don't have to marry her just because she's pregnant," she said, saving her more devout Catholic expressions for the next time she was in public. I imagined that in her best-case scenario, I'd run off to Europe or die during childbirth, leaving Jason no choice but to move back home and have her raise the child with him.

My family was less interested in raising my child for me.

"I'm too young to be a grandparent, Jenny. I'm a mere child myself," my mom whined as a seventeen-year-old spray-tan technician instructed her to bend over and spread her ass cheeks.

But to their credit, both my parents warmed to the idea once they realized that the baby's father was successful and stable and not the guy I rear-ended at Rite Aid.

Jason and I spent the next three months preparing for parenthood. We moved in together, went to couple's therapy, bought an SUV. The circumstances didn't allow us time to play games. We opened up about our own childhoods and forged pacts about the things we would do differently. We bought books, talked about names, and even looked at pictures of kids online.

But as my hormone levels continued to rise, so did my anxiety. I felt like a caged animal, locked into a life that was thrust upon me. Unlike my fledgling acting career, parenthood happened overnight. Whatever I'd tried to do with my life up to that point was now doomed to sit on the back burner. I was going to be one of those moms—those women with unfulfilled dreams, delusions of grandeur, and a need to lip-synch "Cold Hearted Snake" in their daughter's talent show.

And what about Jason? He was great, but so is everybody when you've been sleeping with them for less than a year. Sometimes I'd look over in bed and imagine all the various threats our relationship might face. What if he fell in love with someone more successful than me? What if he fell in love with someone skinnier than me? What if one day he decided he was trans and transitioned into a skinnier, more successful version of me?

My anxiety came to a boil one afternoon on our way to a routine doctor's visit. We were in the SUV, and Jason had turned left on Beverly instead of right. The faster way would have been taking La Cienega to Third, but after living in Los Angeles for almost eleven years, Jason still couldn't tell Third and Beverly apart. When we first met I found his handicap cute, but once I was pregnant, I saw it as a personal affront to my sanity. That would have been enough; then he mentioned that he liked the name "Ernie" for our child-to-be.

"Let me out of the car! I don't even know you! You've completely hijacked my life! I want my life back!" I tried jumping from the SUV.

"Sit down! Jenny, sit the fuck down now!" He tried to hold me in place by the hood of my sweatshirt. His breath smelled like matzo brei to my expectant nostrils as I bit down hard on his hand. The truth was, no matter how serious or ridiculous our fights seemed in the moment, they really didn't matter. Like two siblings bickering in the backseat on a family road trip, we were tethered to each other for eternity, regardless of the outcome.

But at the doctor's office that day, things took an alarming turn. We huddled together on a white exam table covered in crinkled-up paper. The doctor had already exited, giving us a moment alone to digest the news. After three months inside my womb, our fetus had decided to pull the rip cord. His heart had stopped. I was miscarrying.

Before I knew it, I was reclining in a dark room at a nearby clinic, where a giant DustBuster was inserted up my vagina and my fetus and his vacated condo were suctioned out. The fear and anxiety (even the rancid smell of Jason's breath), all of it faded to the background. Once the procedure was complete, Jason and I locked bodies and started crying. I'm not sure we knew everything we were crying for. Our lives, which had been moving so fast, suddenly came to a grinding halt. Our destinies, which a moment before seemed so certain, so cemented together, were without warning ripped apart.

This was my chance. If I needed an exit, I could make one. But the only place I wanted to run was straight to Jason. I couldn't live without him. I mean, I obviously totally could have and I'm sure would have rebounded and been totally fine. But I didn't want to. When I was afraid to love him, he loved me with total conviction. When I questioned my own strength, he trusted me completely. He was either the most incredible man I'd ever known or even more batshit insane than I was. Either way, he was perfect for me.

After committing to carrying Jason's child, the idea of marriage and the idea of Jason no longer scared the shit out of me. (Especially once I confirmed that he looked terrible in a DVF wrap dress.) We eloped that week.

Five incredible years of marriage later, the only name Jason was desperate to transition into was "Dad." I didn't wake up one day and suddenly know I was ready to try again for a baby. But Jason reminded me that I was thirty-four and a half, which was basically thirty-five, which was basically forty, which was WAY past dead, and I figured it was now or never.

Getting pregnant this time around wasn't nearly as easy, partially because the universe never cooperates when you need it to, and partially because figuring out when you're ovulating requires an understanding of second-grade math. I'd spent a solid year halfheartedly fucking around with thermometers and period-tracking apps for my iPhone when my sister insisted I try using a digital ovulation stick. Three months of dragging my heels and getting waylaid by online sample sales later, I finally bought one. Twenty-eight days after that, I was pregnant.

Once again, I fell into my lap hyperventilating, but this time it was with nervous excitement. I didn't feel any more prepared or any less afraid. The only thing I knew with confidence was that with Jason, I was okay having my life hijacked.

At forty-one and a half weeks pregnant, I changed my mind again. And decided that a baby was definitely the wrong choice for me.

"Wait, I might not be ready for children," I said one evening as I waddled around the bedroom, trying to reposition what felt like a tiny knee digging into my rib cage.

"Well, get ready," Jason said, unmoved and far too used to my neurosis.

Logically, I understood that there was someone just underneath the surface of my skin about to explode into the world like the most rewarding zit of all time, but I wasn't feeling connected to him. He kind of seemed like a dick, up all night doing flip-flops around my stomach, probably breaking shit and tagging my uterus with question marks because we hadn't yet decided on his name. His hands defiantly covered his face in every 3-D ultrasound we tried to snap of him. He wasn't even out of my body and already he seemed to be saying, "Get away from me," but also, "Give me your undivided attention forever." Once we met I was sure he'd explain that it was all a misunderstanding and that he had no idea how young and beautiful I was and we'd fall madly in love—or would we? I still couldn't conceive of ever caring about anyone more than my dogs (especially if he had to be washed more than once a month).

The truth was, having kids still worried me; but while I was worried for myself, I was more worried for my son. I knew that no matter what I did, I was bound to fuck *something* up. Every parent is the reason their child eventually spends thousands of dollars in therapy. That I understood. But I didn't want to cause him pain. I didn't want to make mistakes. I didn't want to do anything that would result in my being sent to voicemail for the rest of my life.

Aside from doing my best, there was no real way to predict the outcome. He was going to be his own person with his own point of view, which I'd obviously try to shape heavily, but at the end of the day the ball was going to be in his court. If he wanted to hurt me, he could. I was going to love him too much to maintain any control. I hadn't even met him yet and already this was the most fucked-up relationship I'd ever been in.

I was due on February 4. On February 14, I was still pregnant.

"This is just my new body. It's just what I look like now," I explained to Jason, defeated. I gave him a kiss on the lips and hoisted myself into bed, utterly disappointed.

The truth was that after eight hours of sequestering myself at home and watching *House of Cards*, I'd stopped believing in God and the order of all things. I was over being patient, waiting for nature to take its course. "Fuck nature," I said straight to an imaginary camera in my best Frank Underwood voice. This pregnancy had gone on so long that now my Aquarian son was dangerously close, like three days shy, of becoming a Pisces. I hated Pisces men. All of my exes were Pisces, and they were all overly sensitive, elusive liars. It was such a Pisces move to blatantly ignore my wants and needs and just hibernate in my womb long enough to become a Pisces. I wasn't going to let this happen, I was having an Aquarius even if it meant reaching inside and pulling that little water bearer out myself.

My hair was a teased rat's nest of restlessness. My fingers looked like mini–French baguettes. I rolled myself up on a body pillow like an enslaved Sea World orca and tried to fall asleep.

As I flipped on my side, my water broke.

"Baby . . . I think my water just broke."

"WHAT!? Shouldn't we be drenched? I don't see anything!" He looked up at the sky, expecting a giant bucket of *You Can't Do That on Television* slime to drop from the ceiling and cover us.

"Maybe you just peed," he offered as he searched the sheets for proof.

"Baby, I would know if I just peed, and I didn't. You need to call the doctor." I hurried to the bathroom and stripped off my clothes to make sure I couldn't see a head or the face of one of my former Pisces ex-boyfriends peeking out.

Jason called our doctor, Howie Mandel (his real name), as I sat on the toilet, regretting having used all my pregnancy books as nightstand coasters. I guess I should have prepared myself better, but those books made me feel like I was studying for the SAT. When Howie said I should go back to bed and try to sleep, I was skeptical. I'd *tried* to go to sleep and instead I wet my pants. This time, who knew what might happen? (Of course *I* didn't. See above, re: coasters.) So instead of sleep, I wandered around the house, moaning and groaning. I figured that if I went through the motions of giving birth vocally, my body would eventually catch up. Like in acting class, where they teach you that if you start breathing really fast, eventually you'll burst into hysterics and become Meryl Streep.

Around 3:30 a.m., I gave up and Jason and I drove to the hospital. I wasn't feeling any cramping, but pretended to be miserable, just in case I suddenly felt like screaming or beating Jason uncontrollably and needed an excuse. The streets were empty, save for a couple police cars. Part of me hoped one might try to pull us over, just so I could say, "Sorry, Officer, we don't have time for your bullshit! WE'RE HAVING A FUCK-ING BABY!" then hit the gas and peel out—but no luck.

Once at the hospital, we were escorted into a private delivery suite where I was told to strip. I'd brought no less than seven sexy nightgowns with me. I wasn't sure what kind of message I wanted to send to my newborn son as he emerged into the world. I could be *bohemian silk kimono* mom, *black mesh Agent Provacateur* mom, *lacy, demure floor-length* mom, or even *all white cotton coed* mom. Like a bride at a Kennedy wedding, I assumed I'd probably change twice. I wasn't sure how labor worked, but everyone said it took forever. I told Jason to notify me when he felt we'd hit the halfway point so I could sneak off and slip into my second look.

Before I had a chance to make a nightgown selection, a nurse came in and fingered me. Then another, then another. Suddenly I wasn't feeling very sexy. The final nurse hooked me up to a monitor, where Jason could visibly see that my contractions hadn't actually started and that any sounds I might have been making were only because I thought I was Meryl Streep. I was barely two centimeters dilated when Howie Mandel and my doula, Ana Paula, arrived.

Ana Paula was the type of woman who takes a lot of deep breaths and talks about chakras. She was serene and centered. I'd never seen her car, but I already knew it was a Prius with a bumper sticker that urged fellow drivers to free Tibet. She'd been referred to me by a friend who was shocked that at seven months pregnant, the only thing I had planned out about my birth was the outfits. I finally got around to meeting Ana Paula when I hit thirty-six weeks.

"So, what is your birth plan?" she asked, sitting on my couch, staring inquisitively at the giant photograph on our wall of a small Asian girl holding a bloody butcher knife in one hand and a dead goldfish in the other.

"My plan? Um. Well, I guess at this point I'm having it."

Ana Paula smiled empathetically and promised if I listened to her, I'd have "a magical experience I'd cherish forever."

This was my first time seeing her since our chat, and already I was regretting inviting someone into the room that believed experiences could be magical without drugs.

Howie ordered me a Pitocin drip to help induce labor. He then offered me an epidural. I wasn't opposed to painkillers, per se. But the latest craze in the mommy world was to do things naturally—as opposed to when my mother had kids and the trend was to push the button on your morphine drip as many times as you could before a person sprang from your giant hairy vagina. Also, I'd recently seen that Ricki Lake documentary that persuades all women to give birth in their bathtubs. Though I eventually decided against a home birth, I was still open to the idea of doing things naturally. Mostly just so I could gloat to my mother.

But that was when I was the kind of pregnant that looks

cute in tight shirts and leggings—when I was safe and pain-free in the comfort of my own bed. Now, with what felt like a thousand teeth clenching down on my abdomen, following in my mother's footsteps seemed like a pretty sensible option. I knew Jason and Howie didn't give a shit whether I delivered naturally.

But there was Ana Paula. She favored the holistic approach. She'd delivered countless babies in bathtubs. And even though I knew it shouldn't matter, I needed to know that Ana Paula loved me more than those other babies, that she respected me even without a silk kimono, and she considered me just as strong as the girl that referred her to me. So the drugs would have to wait.

I wandered the halls of the Labor and Delivery ward for five hours, riding the vicissitudes of the most incomprehensible pain of my life. I couldn't stand up straight, I couldn't speak, I couldn't see. My hands were shaking and my back was drenched in sweat when finally my ego was beat into submission.

Physical pain had won out over my need for approval. I asked for the works.

An anesthesiologist, who looked roughly the same age as my boob job, walked in and administered an epidural. From that point forward, everything was a blur. I'm told that Howie, Jason, and Ana Paula sat with me for more than seven hours, waiting for my cervix to dilate. It never did. After endless pushing and pooping myself twice, the baby's heart rate began to drop. A C-section was our only option.

I anxiously sobered up as the nurses wheeled me down the hall toward the brightly lit operating room.

"I think we've passed the halfway point," Jason said, appearing next to me in scrubs and taking my hand.

I smiled at him. Or maybe I smiled at the wall. But it was meant for him.

Howie told us we'd be meeting our son in less than ten minutes. All the choices I'd made with my life—the bad haircuts, the questionable workout mix tapes, the Screamin' Semen—came flooding back to me. I was hit with a flurry of unanswerable questions.

Would this little creature love me? Would he approve of me? Would his friends ever consider me hot? Would he ever find a picture of me from middle school with super-thin eyebrows? Or a Facebook post where I vowed to go vegan? Does my OB-GYN realize that one of my vagina lips is longer than the other? Is it weird to ask him to shave a little off while he's down there?

The nurses rolled me from my hospital bed onto the operating table and placed a linen screen just under my chest. Standing next to me, Jason pulled out his camera and waited anxiously. Once the IV drip took hold, everything below my ribs went numb. I told Howie to let me know before he started cutting.

"We've already started," he said matter-of-factly.

I tried to stay focused and not picture all the balloon animals he might be making out of my intestines and abnormally long pussy lip.

"Okay, you are going to feel a lot of pressure," he instructed.

I waited for a minute, but before I could get super-cocky about not even flinching, I heard a baby cry.

My narcotized eyes looked up and saw Howie's hands holding a bloodied version of Caesar, from Little Caesars Pizza. He had a large Roman nose, chubby cheeks, and a black toupee stuck to his head.

"Pizza pizza," I could have sworn I heard him say as he was whisked off for a bath.

A few minutes later, a nurse walked him back over and placed him on my chest. He seemed a little pissed off. Like maybe the cesarean was interfering with whatever plans he'd made for the evening. I cradled him in my arms the way I'd seen people hold babies in movies, trying to console him.

My heart heaved with emotion as I looked into his dark blue eyes. I wanted to laugh, sob, and throw up all over myself, all at once. I'd burst through the ceiling of any love I'd felt before and was now traveling into the stratosphere reserved for heroin junkies and people who write romantic greeting cards. I didn't recognize these feelings in myself. I was instantly and completely transformed. For once I wasn't thinking about my career or if my hospital smock made me look fat. Yes, I'd make mistakes, and yes, one day my son might decide to send me to voicemail. But it was part of an emotional, painful, joyous journey I was finally happy to take.

I wasn't ready for kids. I was just ready for him.

2

THE CURIOUS INCIDENT OF THE NIGHT NURSE IN THE DAYTIME

I wanted a night nurse because everybody told me I wanted one. A night nurse is basically a woman who lives in your house and tends to your newborn child alongside you. She is on the clock twenty-four/seven, and the majority of her job happens once you are tucked in bed, sleeping soundly through the night, while your baby is screaming his head off because he's no longer floating around in his own subdermal hot-tub time machine. My sister had assured me that the first weeks after bringing Sid home were going to suck. Every couple hours, an adorable little atomic bomb would go off and all hell would break loose. Sid would be angry, he would be hungry, and he would want to know where the fuck I was. The night nurse's job was to attend to his cries, pick him up, change him, and bring him directly to my tit.

Some people might consider this a job for their mothers, especially people who hadn't met mine. I knew my mom was technically more than qualified—she was an RN, after all. But because I *had* met my mother, I felt a little more comfortable serving my tits up to a complete stranger. After the emotional roller coaster of childbirth, I needed stability. Adding my mom to the mix seemed like booking myself an extended ride on Space Mountain. She was well-meaning and fun, but indifferent when it came to genuine angst and/or screaming in the dark.

I was introduced to my first night nurse by Hollice, a woman I'd taken to referring to as my high school rival. I didn't know we were high school rivals at the time—it was only years after college, when she informed me that as kids, she fucking hated me. I was flattered. I guess I'd hated her, too, but I also loved her. We hung out in different circles but shared a common goal: to be the lead in every high school play. I suppose I had talked some shit about her, in the throes of adolescent angst. But I talked shit about everyone. I still do. It's just something that comes naturally. Like doing the splits or knowing the exact whereabouts of my husband's ex. I was jealous of Hollice because she'd done community theater since the age of six and was in a commercial for the local rec center.

Beyond that, I couldn't stand how invested her mom was in her success. Hollice had one of those typical stage moms who lived vicariously through their daughters because their own dreams had never been realized. Hollice's mom knew all the words to every musical number she performed. She waited backstage with notes and feedback, sometimes even a few constructive criticisms for me.

"Jenny, you seemed a little pitchy up there tonight. Is your father getting another divorce?" she asked, feigning concern.

"Probably." I brushed past her, trying to avoid any deep conversation.

"Oh. Sorry to hear that . . . Don't know if Hollice mentioned it, but she just signed with John Casablanca!" she called out proudly.

My mom had never even seen me in a play, but she once dated a guy named John Casablanca. I think he was a child molester. As much as I longed for a cheerleader like Hollice's mom, I knew it couldn't have been easy for Hollice. The anxiety radiated off her. When she entered a room you could feel the pressure, the burden of expectation to fulfill not just her own goals but also her mother's. As a result, Hollice had a depth the other girls didn't. I was drawn to her pain and yet repelled at the same time, because I knew we were fighting inverse battles. Her mother's love was conditional and my mother's was ephemeral. Our experience of our mothers, hers driving her on, mine leaving me grasping for attention, pitted us against each other more than any casting decision could. In a parallel universe we might have been friends, but in this universe, *Grease* has only one Sandy, and we were both too driven to end up beauty school dropouts.

Unlike me, Hollice did become a successful actress. At nineteen, she left college to start working full-time on a CBS sitcom. Meanwhile, I was auditioning for student films with head shots taken by a guy I met at Trader Joe's who offered to waive his fee if he could shave my pussy. It wasn't *what* Hollice was doing so much as what it represented that killed me. Her life was what my life could have become, what it should have been. No matter how hard I tried to be above it, her success served to highlight my failure. Once I'd settled into adulthood, my competitive feelings toward Hollice waned. Partially because

I'd matured, but mostly because I'd found new people to compare myself to.

Hollice had two boys several years older than Sid, and she reached out to me while I was still pregnant.

"Why is she texting me?" I asked Jason, hoping he had the answer.

"To be nice?"

"Why would she want to be nice? She's my nemesis. She's supposed to be rooting for my demise in life."

He laughed. "Jenny, that was years ago. I think she's over you."

"Like over me because I never made it? That's so fucked-up to say!"

"I didn't say it. You did." Exhausted by my insecurities, Jason delicately explained to me that some people do grow up. Not me. But other people.

Hollice seemed sincere. I couldn't help but respect her willingness to offer an olive branch and cautiously decided to give our fake friendship a real chance. And by real, I mean totally fake.

As Hollice and I spent more time together (read: became Internet friends who don't actually hang out) I learned that she was a hands-on mom, the kind of über-competent parent who sculpts things out of fondant and uses a special nontoxic plant-based solution to clean off her fruits and veggies. She'd done her child-rearing homework and was quickly becoming an Instagram authority on the subject. As a childhood development expert, Hollice was a firm believer in the necessity of a night nurse.

"It takes a village," she posted, under a picture of herself and another woman wearing aprons, covered in what looked like baby diarrhea.

According to Hollice, Debora saved her life when she had her second child. She traveled with her all over the globe; she trained the baby to sleep through the night; she even gave Hollice's husband reflexology massages. I wasn't half as busy as Hollice was. But I did love the idea of not having to rub Jason. Hollice had high expectations when it came to caregiving. She was the type of woman who, if she had the time, would have been doing it all herself. If somebody was good enough for Hollice, she was good enough for me.

I hired Debora for six weeks, sight unseen.

I carefully transported Sid home from the hospital on a Sunday. A nurse helped us out to the car and strapped his eight-pound body safely into his car seat. I was too anxious to focus on the myriad belts and levers and feared that once we were home, I might have to use scissors to cut him out. With each twist and turn in the road my anticipation grew. Jason slowly coasted into our driveway like we were burglars prepping for a robbery. Once we were parked and the emergency brake was on, we hopped out of the car and rushed around to the backseat. Sid was still breathing. Jason didn't spend time trying to figure out the buckle situation and instead left Sid content in his carrying case. He unhooked the thirty-pound pod and walked urgently toward the front door as if he were holding a water balloon.

For the last month of my pregnancy our house had been in a state of entropy. Mismatched body pillows and blankets sprawled lazily across every couch, piles of unopened gifts barricaded the kitchen from the dining room, and every glass surface was streaked with cocoa-butter fingerprints.

It was the next day, a Monday, when the doorbell rang signaling Debora's arrival. The dogs went crazy. Jason ran around, tidying up like an eighteen-year-old whose parents were coming home from vacation early. Apprehensively, I hobbled toward the door, nursing my C-sectioned stomach. I had an idea of what was waiting for me on the other side, but I was starting to get cold feet. With Sid out of my uterus, I suddenly felt too emotional to want another person in my home. I wanted to hibernate. I wanted to make a giant nest out of all the hair wrapped around my round brush and bury the two of us deep inside it. I wanted to open my mouth and swallow his little body whole, landing him back in my belly where he belonged.

Taking a deep breath, I worked up the courage to crack open the door.

A tall black woman with a Halle Berry haircut and wearing blue hospital scrubs and large round sunglasses stood there, typing on her cell phone.

"I was afraid I might have the wrong place." Debora smiled sweetly, rolling past me with three matching Louis Vuitton suitcases. "Where's the little yummy?" she said eagerly.

"Who?"

"The baby! The yummy-yum-yum!" Debora flung off her sunglasses and walked into the kitchen to wash her hands.

When Jason tiptoed out of the back room with a sleeping Sid, she lit up.

"Da widdle wummy!" she said in a low whisper, toweling off her hands and taking Sid from Jason like a pro.

Jason smiled at me with an overly confident look that said, "I want credit for all of this." Debora settled onto a bar stool with the yummy and we walked through what to expect for the first week. She inquired about my breast-feeding and if I had any previous experience with newborns.

Tears of self-doubt welled up in my eyes as I shook my head *no*. "I haven't even taken the tags off him yet." I guiltily motioned toward the medical bracelet on Sid's ankle like he was an impulse buy I couldn't actually afford.

Jason patted my shoulder, hoping to offer comfort. I wanted to relax, but I was far too anxious. I didn't know how to take care of a baby. I didn't even know how to work our dishwasher. Everything I needed to know about domesticity I was going to have to learn from Debora.

Debora unpacked her bags in the guest bedroom, soon to be Sid's nursery, formerly the Champagne Room (when I'd taken up pole dancing), before that the Zen Den (when I got super into incense and past lives). Debora must have sensed a disturbance in the air. She pulled a large Bible out of her purse and placed it on her pillow.

"Gotta get my daily dose of the Holy Ghost," she said, lifting her hands over her head like she was about to be beamed up through my roof. Hollice had mentioned that Debora was a Pentecostal, and she spent most of the time she wasn't with the baby reading scripture. I didn't mind her zeal. I took it to be a good indicator that she wouldn't try to murder me in my sleep or order any porn On Demand.

I watched as she laid out towels and created a makeshift

changing station next to the bed. She sprinkled lavender oil in Sid's bassinet and organized his swaddles by color. She asked me how I knew Hollice.

"We've been great friends for years and lost touch for a while because of our booming careers," I lied.

"She's incredible. Truly one of the best people I've ever met."

"Is she?" My voice cracked slightly. I felt a surge of adolescent jealousy.

"Oh, yes. We had the greatest time together. Watched Wendy Williams and *E! News* every afternoon. Got manis and pedis every Friday. Best boss I've ever had."

Huh. I wondered if Debora was just trying to play me for free manicures, but her face seemed sincere. Was it possible that Hollice was the best boss ever? In my mind I liked to picture her life having a dark underbelly. Not that she was Mommy Dearest, but at least that she was a high-maintenance, demanding narcissist whose early success would one day shrivel away with her youth, leaving her washed up and alone like Norma Desmond. I rocked back and forth in my glider, internally grappling with the idea that Hollice was a good person.

"We still text all the time," she continued, as she wrapped her head in a do-rag. "I mean, I lived with her for four months. You just get close." She flashed me a picture of her and Hollice clinking wineglasses on an Air France flight to Saint Bart's.

I smiled and excused myself to have a word with Jason, who was upstairs, ostensibly hanging out with Sid but actually naked on the toilet, answering e-mails.

"We need to hire Debora for at least four months," I insisted. I needed to prove to Debora not only that we were as financially secure as Hollice, but that I was way more fun and totally more right for the role of Medea in our senior-class play.

"You want a stranger in our house for four months?"

"What's the big deal? We already have one that's staying for eighteen years," I said. " 'Of all creatures that can feel and think, we women are the worst treated things alive,' " I moaned, channeling my best mid-Atlantic dialect.

"Isn't *Medea* about a woman who hates her husband and kills her kids?" Jason finished peeing, then traipsed into the bedroom and turned on a golf game.

"And her husband's name was Jason. I would have been brilliant!" I blocked the television and took a long, drawn-out dancer's bow, then pretended to drink a vial of poison, which had nothing to do with the plot of *Medea* and everything to do with showcasing the "Special Skills" section of my résumé that listed my proficiency in mime. Sid watched from a makeshift pillow crib in the center of our bed, clearly picturing what his life would be like if Hollice were his mom.

Jason consented to keeping Debora on for an additional ten weeks, less because he agreed with me and more to increase his odds of never seeing me mime again.

I was quickly learning that a baby is a gift that requires a million other gifts. No matter how prepared you think you are, you are missing at least a dozen vital basics.

"Where are his pajamas?" Debora rummaged through Sid's drawers, confused. It was Sid's first real bedtime in his nursery and the only thing he had on was a diaper and an umbilical cord.

"What do you mean?"

"The baby needs something to sleep in."

"Don't we just swaddle him? I didn't know they made baby pajamas."

"Yes, he *has* to have clothes to sleep in," she said, like a worried social worker talking to a teen mom. "And you also have to buy a bathtub, a bottle warmer, some diaper-rash cream, crib sheets, storage bins . . ."

The list went on and on. I was the least prepared parent she'd ever worked with, she said with an uncomfortable laugh. She told me she'd spoken to her best friend Uzo about the situation during a break that afternoon, and they were going to pray for me on their Tuesday-night prayer hotline. I envisioned her and Uzo on their hands and knees, weeping to Lord Jesus to save Sid from the certain doom that would come from having a mother who was too dumb to know what baby pajamas were and was still hiding a stripper pole in the garage.

Uzo was Debora's good friend who she never shut up about. She also happened to be Beyoncé's baby nurse.

"She's been a celebrity baby nurse for years," Debora said, pulling a bag of kale out of the fridge to make a green drink she'd read about in *Us Weekly*. "She gets paparazzied all the time. You've definitely seen her in all the magazines." Debora beamed. The blender begrudgingly chewed up the copious amounts of ice, almond milk, and bananas as Debora stared at me, waiting for some sort of kudos for the fact that she drank smoothies.

It weirded me out how wrapped up in the fame game my baby nurse was. I understood a hairstylist caring about celebrity—a trainer, even a chef. But a fucking baby nurse? Was there anyone in Los Angeles not trying to jockey their way into their own reality show? Debora was a churchgoing woman, a disciple of the Lord, a woman who told me at least twice a day that she could communicate with angels. But even Debora couldn't resist the siren song of Bravo Andy.

Hollice had taken to texting me daily, checking in. She was over-the-top sweet, asking when she could come over and meet Sid. She'd never been to my house before and I was more than a little hesitant to have her over. I didn't know how I would handle being around her. In high school I had always left our interactions feeling depressed and inadequate. I was afraid even now to hear about what new job she had or what cool friends she was hanging out with. Also I looked like shit. I'd just had a baby and was twenty pounds overweight, with nipples the size of rice cakes.

I told Hollice that I would love to see her! That I couldn't wait! But that, sadly, Jason was experiencing postpartum depression. I suggested we touch base again in a few weeks, hoping her super-glamorous lifestyle would sweep her out of town and prevent our meet-up from ever actually happening. It wasn't that I disliked her. I just wanted to prevent myself from getting hurt or possibly deciding to change Sid's name to something flashy and attention-grabbing like "Afrika" to ensure he'd be more famous than her kids.

"Hollice might stop by in a few weeks to say hi," I casually mentioned one morning as I loaded Sid into his car seat. We were going for a routine doctor's visit in West L.A. and Jason had asked Debora if she wanted to join us. We didn't know how not to. Leaving her in the house alone all day just seemed rude.

Debora had been at our house just under a month at that point, and she was already way too comfortable with us. It wasn't all her fault. Jason and I didn't know how to say no. Neither of us had grown up with "staff," and bossing an older black woman around the house just felt a little too *Gone with the Wind*. So instead of treating Debora like an employee, we treated her like a houseguest. I stocked the house with everything she liked to eat: berries, tortilla chips, coconut water. I bought her a bathrobe and a down comforter. I even let her borrow my car when she needed to run errands. Some people know how to handle obvious codependents like Jason and me, and they would have likely compensated for our lack of boundaries by enforcing boundaries of their own. But others tend to take advantage of our hospitality and end up controlling us completely.

I can't deny that part of why I let it happen was to ensure that Debora enjoyed her stay with me more than she did her stay with Hollice.

"Can we eat at Mr Chow?" Debora chimed in from the backseat as we made our way to the doctor. "Uzo always gets to go to Mr Chow."

Mr Chow was a high-end Chinese restaurant in Beverly Hills that I hadn't eaten at since the early nineties. Once a notorious hotspot to see and be seen in, Mr Chow had in recent years become little more than a tourist trap (with great lettuce cups) and a standard stop for every TMZ tour bus.

"Maybe . . ." I said, annoyed, looking at Jason from the passenger seat. I'd spent enough time around her to realize that whenever Debora really wanted to get her way, she'd throw a little Jesus talk into her negotiating.

"The Lord Jesus is telling me I gotta get me some Mr Chow! Because the Lord was not liking what you fed me last night." She paused, reading a text on her phone, then continued, half-focused. "The only kind of sushi I can do is a Californian roll."

Not only was Debora strangely manipulative, she was always on her phone. And aside from the handful of times I'd heard her wiring money to a relative in Atlanta, she was usually gossiping with Uzo.

Uzo was the Queen Bee of the baby-nurse world. She was the Heather with the red scrunchie. She had an army of lower-level baby nurses she'd farm jobs out to when she deemed them unworthy of her time. Uzo seemed like a self-obsessed fame whore. And though she'd unequivocally signed a nondisclosure agreement with her current employer, she didn't mind bending the rules to divulge secrets, especially if it allowed her to brag about a fancy new trip or a restaurant she'd tried. Debora worshipped Uzo and wanted everything she had. This included "the three *b*'s."

"My goals are simple," she said, sucking down garlic prawns at Mr Chow after our appointment. "I want a Bentley, a black card, and a Birkin. Then I'll know I've made it."

I didn't own a black card, nor a Bentley, and I most definitely didn't own a Birkin. With prices ranging anywhere from ten to two hundred grand, a Birkin was an outrageously priced handbag typically reserved for Park Avenue princesses. Out of principle, I couldn't imagine myself ever buying one. But I did take note when someone around me had one. Carrying a Birkin is like the female version of walking into a locker room with a monster-sized dick. Eyes turn in your direction; perceptions shift. When I see a Birkin on the street, I eye it the way I do a girl who's prettier than me. It's a mixture of jealousy, lust, and begrudging respect. I try to guess if the owner bought the bag herself or if she's just letting someone else's husband come in her mouth. If she looks at me, I smile. I even offer my help if needed. No matter how hard I try to fight it, I'm disarmed, subservient, and mildly depressed.

I stared out at two grungy-looking paparazzi standing near the valet. They waved to a Hollywood tour bus filled with sunburnt white people in visors.

"I don't have any of those things," I said to Debora, trying to bring her back down to earth.

"Uzo got a Céline from Beyoncé for her birthday. My birthday is next week. I'm about to be fifty! That's a big birthday." Debora let the information hang in the air as a waiter walked over and handed Jason the check. "You're only fifty once, after all," she said, as if you're other ages more than once.

"Oh, I think I wanna order something for later." Debora looked at us innocently. She told the waiter she'd like the lobster pasta and another order of shrimp toast to go. Jason shot me a look, then gave the waiter his credit card.

"You've got one of them Célines, though . . ." Debora said. She'd clearly been digging through my closet while I was out.

"It's a knockoff," I shot back, defensive. "I got it in Turkey. Jason, tell her it's a knockoff."

"It's a knockoff," Jason said, handing me Sid and excusing himself to the bathroom.

"I actually have a fake Birkin, too," I confessed under my breath. "I got it from my guy Elan here in town. I just can't justify spending all that money on real bags. I don't care about them enough."

Debora looked at me, shocked. Her jaw hung open. I could see bits of macerated shrimp waving at me between her teeth. "You carry a fake bag?"

"Well, yeah. Sometimes."

The truth was I loved fake bags. They provided me with all the respect and credit that comes with a real bag for a fraction of the cost.

"I could NEVER. Debora don't break for fake!" She threw an arm in the air for emphasis.

Debora and I walked with Sid out toward the valet. The paparazzi were still waiting, to Debora's satisfaction. She giddily applied lipstick and grabbed Sid from my arms. I smiled at the two broken men with beat-up jeans and telescope lenses as they scanned my face through their mental database, coming up with absolutely zero reason to take my picture.

"Weird. They aren't shooting us." Debora shrugged, disappointed. "When I was with Hollice people basically attacked us for photos."

I felt a pang of defeat in the pit of my stomach. I knew Debora was judging me. *I* was judging me. Just then, Jason appeared and the men sprang into action.

"Quick, Debora! Go hold his hand!" I heard myself say. "Give him a peck on the cheek! See if he'll dip you!" The words poured out of my mouth. It was as if the Holy Ghost had inhabited my body, only instead of speaking in tongues I was speaking in Kardashian.

Jason gave Debora an awkward, obligatory hug, then jumped into the car, rattled. We didn't speak about the incident until later that night.

"I couldn't disappoint her! She wanted it so badly. Uzo bullies her and makes her feel like she's not a high-profile-enough baby nurse, it's just not fair!" I said, like a mom talking about her overweight teenage daughter.

Jason looked at me in disbelief. "Do you hear yourself? 'High-profile-enough baby nurse'? What does that even mean? She's here to take care of our kid. She's lucky we even take her out of the house."

"Jason! That's racist!"

"Racist? I don't care what color skin she has. We aren't here to improve her social status."

"Yes, we are!" I said, realizing the absurdity only after the words had come out.

In my heart, I knew Jason was right, but I couldn't help myself. Debora was Patrick Dempsey from *Can't Buy Me Love*. She was Rachael Leigh Cook from *She's All That*. She was the DUFF from *The DUFF*. I related to her feelings of inferiority. And I felt it my duty to transform her into the coolest girl in school.

Later that night I rocked Sid to sleep while Debora sat in the kitchen eating her ninety-five-dollar lobster pasta. When I walked out, she stopped me.

"So. I thought about what you said and . . . I wanna meet your dealer."

"I—" I hesitated, wondering which dealer she was referring to and how deep she'd actually dug into my closet. "Elan?"

"I prayed about it and I think you are right. Gonna start out with a fake Birkin and work my way up. Hang on." Debora held one hand to my lips while the other went to her ear like a Secret Service agent. "Uh-huh, yeah . . . Okay . . . Yup. I understand." She nodded as she looked off into space, having a conversation with nobody.

Part of me wished Jason were in the room to see her communing with the Lord. The other part of me was relieved because he would have undoubtedly noted that Debora was a better mime than me.

"The Holy Ghost is on board. He wants me to have black caviar leather with gold hardware. Can you take me tomorrow?"

"Umm . . ."

I really didn't want to take Debora to see Elan. In recent months I'd become convinced that I was going to be arrested for buying illegal merchandise from him. I even deleted his number from my cell phone, contacting him only through my friend Adele, who I didn't really care what happened to. But Debora looked desperate and vulnerable and I had a way to help her. I could give her a gift Hollice couldn't provide. It would almost be cruel not to, I reasoned.

The next morning, I called Adele and asked her to set up a meeting with Elan. Adele bitched and whined, less because she minded and more because those were the only noises her mouth was capable of making.

"Why do I have to do all this stuff for you? I'm not your assistant."

"I know. If you were my assistant I'd never feel comfortable taking this much advantage of you."

Adele told me she'd call Elan and call me right back. When my phone vibrated two minutes later, I picked it up without looking at it.

"Hi."

"Hi," a vaguely familiar voice said.

I looked at the caller ID. It was Hollice.

"Hollice! How are you? Sorry, I thought you were somebody else," I said, trying to recover from the awkward pause.

"I'm gonna be in your neighborhood next week for a meeting and I have a gift I wanna drop off. Does Monday work for you?"

"Yes! That sounds great." I paced around the kitchen, looking for something to stress-eat.

"Cool. Text me directions and I'll swing by around noon. I can even bring lunch."

I graciously accepted and told her we'd speak soon. After I hung up, I took a deep breath, then swallowed a half wheel of Brie. I reminded myself that Monday was a week away and that anything could happen between now and then. Maybe Hollice would have to cancel. Maybe my poodle, Mr. Teets, would get hit by a car. Maybe I'd need an emergency hysterectomy.

Seconds later, Adele called back and told me Elan could be at her work in thirty minutes. Desperate for a distraction, I ran upstairs and threw on a pair of sweats. Sid was asleep on Jason and I asked if it would be okay if we left them alone for an hour. I explained that I had some errands to run and I needed Debora to come with me. A woman might have questioned my motives, but a man tends to accept whatever you tell him if you talk about it fast enough. Jason didn't even raise an eyebrow as I spewed a bunch of nonsense about Gelson's having a sale on kohlrabi, and needing to find an eco-friendly dry cleaner, and the myth of the vaginal orgasm. He nodded and sipped his coffee, counting down the minutes until I shut up.

Debora was ecstatic as we got in the car and headed over to Adele's work. My child was only weeks old and already I'd gone back to work; however, this time it wasn't for myself. I was working for my baby nurse.

We arrived to find Adele waiting outside on a patch of fake grass in front of a large sign that read OCEANA APARTMENTS. She was a leasing agent at the West Hollywood complex (situated nowhere near the ocean), and I'd met her eight years prior when she overcharged me for a one-bedroom with a street-facing bedroom window. Over time we became close friends.

I chose not to write about Adele in my first book because we were in a massive fight at the time. I forget the details of the feud, but I think it originated with me using the back of one of my earrings to lance a cyst between her boobs while she was driving. Normally, I'd be afraid to divulge so much information about a friend, for fear that they might hold it against me later when they saw it in print, but the cool thing about Adele is that she doesn't read. I mean, yes, she *can* read. But she chooses not to because she lacks the attention span. In fact, she still thinks she was mentioned in my first book, so if you happen to see her, please corroborate that story.

Adele was a voluptuous girl with a head of blond spiraled ringlets that framed her olive cheeks like a lion. She was a Jewish American Princess whose Bat Mitzvah theme was "Shopping at Neiman's." At sixteen, her parents bought her a white Volkswagen Cabriolet with the license plate TOY4ADY. When she turned forty, her father finally stopped footing the bill and cut her off financially. With a mountain of growing debt and a wallet full of maxed-out credit cards, Adele had no choice but to sell all her legitimate fancy bags and shoes to her dad's new wife at a fraction of the cost. Once strongly opposed to the idea of fake bags, Adele reconsidered when her means dried up. Now she was not only Elan's toughest critic, she was his best client.

After our introductions, a cream-colored Toyota pulled up. Elan, an older Israeli dressed like Panama Jack, got out of the car.

"Jenny. Long time no talk," he said coquettishly.

I introduced Debora and told Elan to show her all the fake Birkins. He opened up his trunk to reveal a sea of boxes and bags all labeled in Japanese. Reaching into a canvas sack tucked in the far-back corner, Elan pulled out a beautiful black Birkin knockoff.

"It has the authenticity card, the mini-lock, the leather tie," he said. Debora tried the bag on, smiling from ear to ear.

"I love it!"

"It's great, right? Adele? You agree?" I looked over at Adele, who'd crawled inside Elan's trunk.

"I want the new Chanel Boy Bag, but these don't look good enough," Adele bitched, as if the bags' shortcomings were Elan's fault. "Do you have any Givenchy Mini Pandoras?"

"Adele! Get out of the trunk. You don't need another bag," I barked.

Knowing I was right, she pried her fingers free and crawled out of the trunk sheepishly, like a child who just got scolded for opening someone else's birthday gifts. Debora handed her potential purchase to Adele, who held it to the light and scrutinized it closely. "Yeah, it looks good. You should get it."

With Adele's diva stamp of approval, Debora was sold. She paid Elan several hundred dollars cash and we bid him farewell. Adele returned to work and we headed back to Jason and Sid.

The whole ride home, Debora kept peeking into the box at her new purse, worried it might disappear if she didn't check in on it. Everything was right in the world. Debora was filled with joy and I got to be a fairy godmother. If this didn't tip the scales in my favor as "Best Boss Ever," I didn't know what would.

For the next few days, Debora's Birkin sat untouched next to her bed, balanced on her Bible.

"Gotta fake it till ya make it!" became her new motto. I asked her whether she'd told her friends about the bag, but she insisted she hadn't. Every time I checked in on her, I'd find her on the Hermès website.

"Did you know they make a raincoat for the bag? I just bid on one on eBay." Debora moonwalked across the room, pushing her hands up at the ceiling in a "raise the roof" fashion.

I didn't know anything about a Birkin raincoat, but I found it charming that Debora was so invested in decking out her new purse. Like a little girl with a fancy new doll, her excitement was contagious; I couldn't help but indulge her.

"You need to get a scarf now to wrap around it."

"Yaaaasss! I gotta get me a scarf. Maybe something purple."

In the back of my head I started to fantasize about surprising Debora with a purple Hermès scarf for her upcoming birthday. I'd never bought myself anything from Hermès, but now I was as fully invested in Debora's makeover as if it were my own.

Monday rolled around faster than I wanted it to, and there wasn't a dead dog or prolapsed uterus in sight. Hollice was coming over and there was nothing I could do to stop it.

At around twelve-fifteen, the doorbell rang. Again, the dogs went ballistic, and again, Jason ran around the house Pavlovianly straightening things.

"Hollice's here, Yummy!" Debora lifted Sid out of his swing and took him to the front door as if he was about to meet his real mother.

I'd debated all night whether to wear makeup for the visit. I was committed to wearing sweats, because I couldn't have Hollice knowing I was trying too hard to impress her—I didn't want to give away my power so easily. We were on my turf, after all, and I wanted her to feel just as uncomfortable as I did.

In a last-minute stroke of genius, I threw my hair up in a bun, exposing a scar on my forehead that only people who knew me in childhood have really ever seen: a lightly colored T-shaped incision above my right eyebrow, the remaining evidence of a car accident I'd been in at nine years old. The scar wouldn't surprise Hollice; she'd undoubtedly seen it before. I'd even heard rumors that the rec-center commercial would have been mine if it weren't for my mangled mug. Wearing my hair off my face would send a message: I was coming at her from a place of honesty, from a place of vulnerability. Maybe motherhood wasn't just a new chapter for us as women, maybe it was also a new chapter for us as friends.

Debora opened the door and rushed straight toward Hollice without even looking. She embraced her hard, sandwiching Sid's mini-body between them. Hollice looked simple and effortless in a pair of tight-fitting overall shorts and sandals. Her lips were stained coral and her long dark hair was knotted into one of those braids you need an instructional YouTube video to master. Instantly self-conscious about my scar, I tore out my bun and whipped my hair around like a porn star making the transition from uptight secretary to office whore. Then, pretending I needed to pee, I ran upstairs. Jason saw me coming.

"Where are you going?" he asked, cutting me off from the bathroom.

"I just want to get something out of my eye," I said.

"No you don't. You want to put on makeup. Don't do it," he cautioned. "Be the bigger person."

"Don't say that! It makes me sound fat." I brushed past him, frantic.

A few minutes later I walked downstairs in a sundress and a sensible pair of heels. Hollice was busy gabbing with Debora in her room.

"It's so crazy to have you here." I leaned sexily against the door, biting my lips, now fire-engine red.

"Yeah. What a long, crazy journey we've had together, right?" There was no sarcasm, no resentment. She was honest and humble. She asked all about the baby and disclosed how hard it had been for her to breast-feed. She talked about her older son and how jealous he was when the second baby arrived. Hollice wasn't trying to look good. She wasn't trying to compete. She was just being real.

I offered her a drink before we walked back into the living room and sat down. She gave me a blanket she'd crocheted for Sid and a box of sandwiches from her favorite deli. Her generosity, coupled with my estrogen levels, made me want to cry. I was ashamed of all the times I'd felt jealous of her or fantasized about pushing her off a cliff. I didn't address it because in a weird way, I didn't have to. She already knew. Our acknowledgment of the past was unspoken, and whatever issues we'd previously brought up for each other were for the most part absolved.

Just as my defenses started to drop, I heard a scream from Debora in the back room. Hollice leapt out of her seat. I followed.

When we got to her room, Debora was on the phone, shrieking.

"Grandma! You are in the hospital? No-No-NOOOOOO!" she cried, with a blood-curdling scream. Like a loose tampon in a purse, she'd come undone.

Hollice grabbed Debora's hand as she started sobbing. Reflexively I grabbed her other hand to show that I was just as invested in her meltdown as Hollice was.

Debora held the phone in the crook of her neck and continued. "Okay, Grandma, we gonna pray. Dear Lord Heavenly Father, I'm not asking you for ninety-three, not ninety-four, not ninety-five, I'm asking you for a huuuuuuuuundred years, sweet Jesus!" Debora's eyes rolled to the back of her head as she swayed like an Evangelical preacher. Finally she hung up and buried her face in Hollice's chest.

"You know Grammy, Hollice. I think we're gonna lose her."

"You need to go to her. Do you want me to drive you?" Hollice offered.

"I can also drive you." I made a feeble attempt to make my lip quiver with concern while trying to wedge my way back into the conversation.

THE CURIOUS INCIDENT OF THE NIGHT NURSE

"No. I gotta go alone." Debora directed her words to her former boss, instantly composed.

"Well, I don't think you should drive," Hollice said maternally.

"I'll get you an Uber!" I interjected, even more maternal.

Hollice insisted Debora take me up on the Uber, and she agreed. I ordered an SUV, less for Debora than for Hollice. Debora went to the fridge and grabbed a Pellegrino before walking outside to wait for her ride.

Once she left, Hollice and I shared a look.

"Umm . . . What just happened?"

"She always did have a flair for the dramatic." Hollice sighed.

"Yeah, she's been great but . . . a little high-maintenance?" I cautiously tested the waters. After seeing how close they were, I had to choose my words carefully.

"Well, Jenny. When you buy someone a Birkin, it sort of sets the tone," she teased.

"What was I supposed to do? She demanded one!"

"Jenny, I'm famous and I don't even own a real Birkin," Hollice said, suddenly serious.

The words "Jenny, I'm famous" cut so deep that I was momentarily unable to ingest the ones that followed. I paused for a beat before looking at Hollice, confused.

"It's not real. I took her to my fake-bag guy." I stopped myself short, suddenly realizing that telling Hollice I took Debora to my fake-bag guy was also telling Hollice I had a fake-bag guy.

"What do you mean? The Birkin is fake? She told everyone it's real and that you got it for her. I heard about it through my friend Beyoncé. Debora is friends with her baby nurse." She said it nonchalantly, as if being friends with Beyoncé was the most natural thing ever. As if she didn't want me to confuse *her* friend Beyoncé with any other Beyoncés I might possibly know—like Beyoncé the dog groomer or Beyoncé the Rite Aid cashier or any of the many Beyoncés I might be acquainted with from college.

On one hand, I was angry at Debora for spreading the rumor that I bought her such an outrageous gift, which I could now see made me look like a frivolous psychopath. On the other hand, I was pissed that I'd outed myself to Hollice—now she knew *my* Birkin was a fake. Why had Debora put me in such an uncomfortable position? Hadn't she suspected that lying to Uzo would get back to her? Was she that desperate for approval?

I glanced down at my phone, which was flashing me a notification that Debora had arrived at her destination. After hearing Hollice's story, I didn't know what to believe: Did she really get dropped off at the hospital? Was her grandmother really sick? Was she even *alive*?

Hollice encouraged me to set the record straight with Debora when she returned. She also promised she would make things right with her friend Beyoncé. I smiled weakly, as Hollice whipped out her phone and shot someone a text.

"You're all good." She looked back up at me and smiled. "I know you really don't want rumors like that going around, but do try to be empathetic when you speak to Debora. Put yourself in her position," Hollice said as she grabbed her things to go. (Probably to Beyoncé's house.)

Debora returned five hours later. She smelled like roast beef and strawberry shake as she explained that, mercifully, Grandma would have to spend only one more night in the hospital before coming home. Apparently, she'd made a full recovery. I probed deeper, asking questions I suspected she wouldn't be able to answer. But the more I pushed, the more elaborate her story grew.

"So you're saying it was a stroke?" I asked.

"They thought so . . . but now maybe not. Since I was in my baby-nurse scrubs they mistook me for a real nurse and had me scrub in to help. I wasn't gonna stop them, since I wanted to be there if anything happened to Grammy. But at the end of the day, I think it was just a love tap from the Lord. A wake-up call for the whole family, you know?"

"No. I don't know," I said sharply, sitting on a bar stool at my laptop, on the verge of making five nonreturnable purchases I was sure to regret.

Debora was unfazed by my frustration. "Uzo called and I made her FaceTime me so she could see me in an SUV. I'm really styling now! Big-time baby nurse, say whaa?" she asked the empty room rhetorically.

I spun around on my bar stool, ready to confront Debora, when I stopped myself. Her face was giddy with joy. She pranced around the room with pride. In that moment I knew exactly why she'd lied—not about Grandma but about the bag. It was the same reason I covered my scar when Hollice came over. I wanted to appear cool, confident, and more like her—or at least how I pictured her.

Maybe Debora and I were the same—okay, she was a tad more pathological and a dash more religious. But at our core, we both just wanted to feel like we were good enough. I understood her feelings of inadequacy too well to be the one to call her out.

Confronting Debora about her lie would only humiliate her. Fake or not, the bag was providing her with some kind of defense against her own inadequacies. Debora wanted the baby-nurse world to think she was good enough to work for some Birkin-buying billionaire the same way I wanted Hollice to believe I had a flawless forehead capable of landing me a Neutrogena campaign. I didn't need to put myself in Debora's shoes to understand her need to feel worthy. I was in those shoes every day. I thought about Hollice and what insecurities she secretly harbored. I replayed our visit in my head, wondering if she felt the need to prove anything to me. Maybe she wasn't even friends with Beyoncé. Maybe the *B* she texted in her phone was actually Bai Ling. I'd likely never know.

As Debora's dancing slowed, I began to see her in a different light. She wasn't ready to accept everything about herself and neither was I. We were both still striving to be something more, something better. And while I knew I couldn't fight her battles for her, I decided that it wouldn't hurt anyone if I affected the outcome of a few small ones.

As I handed the gray-haired sales associate my credit card, I glanced shamefully around the showroom. I saw a sea of status whores of varying ages, snapping pictures of themselves in enamel bangles and large leather totes.

"This is such an elegant indulgence," the woman said as she folded an equestrian-themed purple scarf into a perfect square, then placed it delicately in a sizable bright orange box. "You'll have it forever!" I watched her as she robotically looked at my credit card, trying to guess what I did for a living.

I eyed the receipt, then pulled my hair proudly into a defiant bun and shrugged.

"Well," I said, "you're only fifty once."

3

NILF

fter six straight hours of breast-feeding Sid up and down the aisle of the Airbus A330, my legs were aching and my boobs were as deflated as the oxygen masks in the compartments overhead. From my spot near the lavatories, I could see Jason, who was sleeping helpfully with his face against his tray table. I hoisted Sid up to see his dad's impressive drooling and felt a twinge of something in my right knee.

I'd booked this trip to Hawaii for the three of us earlier that week when it dawned on me that Debora was planning her escape from my life. We'd reached the end of our contracted time together, and by the weekend, she would be moved into a new house with a new Sid and a new set of lactating areolae. For the first time since having a baby, I was going to be on my own.

The vacation was planned a bit impulsively. I generally liked to take my time planning getaways. Unless, of course, I was on Ambien. When Jason and I first got together I remember plenty of times we'd get a knock on the door at six in the morning and a car service would be waiting in the driveway to whisk us off to God knows where. But those days were behind us, mainly because Jason asked me to hide his Ambien prescription from him and I'd forgotten where I'd put it. But I couldn't blame this trip on drugs. (I was still breast-feeding, after all.) This trip was motivated by something stronger. Debora had left our house on a Saturday morning, after living with us for four months, and, crazy or not, I'd grown attached to her. I was comforted by her Black Christian TV shows and exaggerated nursing credentials. I felt safe and protected knowing that whatever happened, I had a self-proclaimed expert on hand twenty-four/seven. Debora's departure signaled the beginning of a new chapter. I was officially somebody's mom, with no role model of my own. I felt like I'd been given the keys to a shiny new sports car, but only because I lied about knowing how to drive a stick. *I didn't fucking know how to drive a stick.* And I certainly didn't know how to take care of a baby. So I acted without thinking. By Monday, Jason, Sid, and I were on a flight bound for Honolulu to see the only person who knew less about children than I did: my mom.

On an intellectual level I knew visiting my mom was a dicey idea. Her lack of maternal instinct was exactly why I'd hired Debora in the first place. That and the fact that I couldn't handle listening to her remind me that in some circles she was now considered a NILF, a "Nana I'd Like to Fuck." But I was petrified, and whether it's healthy or not, primal fear has this uncanny way of driving all of us back to our mothers (even if they're fucking batshit). Despite the years I'd spent being dumped with babysitters, being dumped with my father, and being told she'd never live her life for her kids, I was still hoping that now that she was older, retired, and less fuckable, my mom might see the error of her ways and want to be close to me. Or, if nothing else, I figured we could at least have a few laughs and share a few heartfelt moments the way moms and daughters do in tampon commercials.

From the aisle I looked over at Jason, who was leaning back against his seat now, gently snoring. Jason had been a huge help these past couple months, but he, too, was new to parenthood and slightly too neurotic to instill in me the sense of calm I was looking for. Wrong or right, I needed my mom. So I convinced him to fly to Hawaii by telling him the lie that all new parents hope is true, that parenting is easier on a beach.

For the past five years, my mom and her husband, John, had owned a timeshare on the island of Lanai. According to Wikipedia, Lanai, sometimes referred to as the Pineapple Island, is the sixth largest of the Hawaiian Islands. In other words, it's basically the smallest. I think there might be one or two smaller, but I'm pretty sure they're just inhabited by tropical birds and Lilliputians. Not only was Lanai ideal for rest and relaxation, it was also just small enough to provide my mom with little else to do besides focus on me.

When we landed in Honolulu, Jason gathered up our explosion of belongings and I carried our bloated baby off the plane. Equal parts exhausted and relieved, we made our way through the humid outdoor airport to a smaller terminal, where a prop plane was already waiting for us. We hurriedly boarded the vessel bound for Lanai, eager to reunite with someone on the other side whose arms weren't about to fall off from holding an infant. I felt slightly embarrassed that I'd started to consider a seventeen-pound baby heavy. My college computer weighed more. But I'd recently injured my leg at the gym and the additional weight was taking its toll. When we stood up to disembark our Island Air flight into Lanai Airport, I was limping. As I hobbled through the tiny airport's provisional baggage claim area, my mom and her dog came bounding toward me.

What I'd overlooked in my haste to connect with my mother was one small roadblock: a twelve-pound black-and-white party poodle named Rocky.

Part of becoming an adult means coming to terms with the fact that your mother's dog is living the childhood you always wanted. It's not his fault; he just lucked out and met her in a more enlightened time. She was finally ready for responsibility. She'd had a few trial runs (with me and my sister), killed a few plants, and was at last open to the idea of constantly feeding and watering and wiping someone's ass with baby wipes. Rocky was living the childhood I always wanted. He had my mom's undivided love and attention; they were rarely apart. Unlike Teets, Rocky was a poodle with a pedigree. Both his parents were show dogs, and he was engineered on a breeding ranch in Texas to be the ultimate specimen. To me, Rocky always looked like Michael Jackson wearing eyeliner. They had the same nub of a nose and uneven two-toned skin color. It didn't matter to Rocky if he was black or white, because he was both simultaneously. His legs were atypically long for his body, so every time he moved he looked like he was reenacting the "Thriller" video. Rocky was sweet, but my mom's coddling had made him into one of those high-maintenance basket-case dogs who eat only chopped chicken salad, refuse to set foot on wet grass, and travel with their own body pillow. Part of me hated Rocky and the other part of me respected the fuck out of him. What was he doing that I wasn't? What did he understand that I couldn't? I wanted to study his moves, learn his strategies, and then eventually usurp him.

As soon as my mom saw Sid, she pulled out her iPhone and started snapping pictures.

"What's up with your leg, Choppy? Why are you walking like a pirate?"

My mom had called me Choppy since she'd accidentally guillotined my ring finger in a sliding minivan door when I was eight. "Choppy" didn't refer to the act of trying to cut off my finger, but to "Chop-chop, Jenny," because she felt the entire debacle could have been prevented if I had been moving faster. When her then husband, an orthopedic surgeon named Stew, attempted to sew the top of my finger back to the base, the nurse asked him what kind of dressing he wanted. I yelled, "Ranch, please." The operating room erupted in laughter. It was in that moment that I decided my childhood pain could be cured only by endless approval from strangers.

"I don't know. I think my body is just still messed up from pregnancy," I lied. The truth was, I knew exactly why I was walking like a pirate. I'd started working out again. And instead of easing my way back in like a normal person, I'd taken to running my ass off on the treadmill like I was going through a messy divorce. I knew getting back to my fighting weight was going to take time and I had every intention of being patient with myself.

That was until I looked in a full-length mirror. My hips were wider than they'd ever been, my face looked like I'd gotten stung by a hive of bees, and there was a bulge under my C-section scar that had me convinced my doctor forgot a pair of forceps inside me. I didn't recognize myself. Growing to term had been such a slow process that I'd had time to wrap my head around the idea of wearing bigger jeans and not seeing my vagina. But the transformation from adorably healthy pregnant lady to non-pregnant sloth-monster was overnight. As a society, we grant expectant mothers leniency. We celebrate them and encourage them to flaunt their ripened bellies in bodycon bandage dresses. Up until the second their child hits fresh air. Then, instantly, we turn on them. We judge them. We diminish them. We demand they pull themselves back together, because just looking at them makes us feel hopeless and undesirable.

I tried to accept my new body with grace and confidence, outwardly, while internally shaming myself and struggling to get back to normal. Sometimes at night, I'd stand in the shower feeling like I was wearing seven-millimeter neoprene. My abdomen was still numb and from the side it looked like a mini continental shelf, dropping off sharply just below the bikini line. After a C-section, doctors suggest waiting sixteen weeks before engaging in physically strenuous activities. I was proud of myself for only waiting eight. I would walk into Barry's Bootcamp, loudly tell my instructor to go easy on me because I'd just had a baby, and then haul ass next to whatever physically fit person was on the treadmill next to me. On days when I was feeling particularly rotund, I'd age Sid down to make my waistline look more impressive. With each week I shaved off his age, five pounds of expectation was lifted off my ass. In retrospect, I feel ridiculous for lying, but not enough to not do it again if I had a second kid or a thyroid problem.

My mom and John helped with our luggage while I hobbled to the backseat of their Jeep and strapped Sid in.

"You said you were going easy at the gym," Jason said to me sternly once we were alone in the car.

"I am."

"You are what?" my mom said, hopping in the front seat with Rocky and scrolling through her new pics.

"Happy to be here." I smiled.

"Good! Some Moc time was way overdue!" My mom had taken to calling herself the Moc after my sister made her an Instagram account with the name watermoccasin25. She decided on "watermoccasin" because my mom was a water sign born in the Chinese year of the snake and the water moccasin was the only venomous water snake she could think of. Curiously, my mom took no offense—except just for a minute, after she learned that the water moc has large jowls due to its venom glands. Once she was assured that the nickname wasn't a knock against her looks, she embraced it with enthusiasm. Calling her the Moc was sometimes easier than calling her Mom because it encapsulated the duality of emotions I had toward her. A water moccasin is a fun-time pit viper who enjoys lounging on the beach, skinny-dipping in lakes, and vanishing as soon as its kids are born. Though aggressive only if provoked, a water moc bite could lead to permanent muscle damage, internal bleeding, loss of an extremity, or death.

The five of us headed down the manicured main road lined with Cook Island pines to Manele Bay.

"Don't worry, Sid, I'm deleting all the angles where you look like a total fatso," my mom called over her shoulder.

I looked at Jason. After six years of marriage, he still couldn't help but register shock at the Moc's candor.

"And you wonder why you had an eating disorder," he said under his breath.

When we arrived at the condo, my mom walked us through all the changes she'd made since our last visit. She pointed out the refurbished teak lawn chairs, the marble countertops, and Rocky's custom canopy bed. The bed stopped me in my tracks. I'd always wanted one as a kid, though I'm not sure I'd ever shared that information with my mom, as I was living full-time with my father by the time I was of canopy-bed age.

When my sister and I were eleven and twelve, my mom suggested we leave San Diego and move to Arizona to live with my dad because she didn't think she could handle us anymore. Though devastating at the time, I channeled my feelings of rejection into more productive pursuits, like becoming my dad's girlfriend. By my twenties it was something I could talk about rationally with my therapist (when I wasn't talking about being my dad's girlfriend), self-diagnosing my abandonment issues with an eye-roll and a dismissive laugh. I felt nothing about it because, I told myself, I felt nothing about her.

But I couldn't deny feeling a sting as I locked eyes with Rocky. He probably had the scooter I always wanted, too— and the hot-pink Rollerblades, and the giant lips phone, and the beeper with the clear case. I squeezed Sid's little body like a Capri Sun and walked into the guest bedroom to drink him in, opting out of the tour.

"Choppy! Wait up! This is the best part," she said, like a little kid about to attempt a stunt on the monkey bars. Jason continued without me. My mom was too engrossed in her sconces to notice.

"Sconces can really make or break a room," I heard her say through the wall.

The Moc was always renovating whatever place she currently called home. At least once every six months I'd get an e-mail with pictures of new backsplashes for her kitchen, new tiles for her shower. Each time, she'd become utterly engrossed in the process. And yet, once it was done, she'd inevitably find a reason to shed her skin and move somewhere else. As a child, we moved every year, sometimes to a different state, sometimes just down the block. For as long as I'd known her, my mom's environment was in flux. And in her younger years, this included the players in it. Both as a homeowner and as a woman, she was restless and fickle. She could be the adoring doting parent one minute and a total stranger the next.

I recognize some of the same instincts in myself. Like her, I too have a track record of cutting relationships short, keeping people at arm's length, trying to outrun my own vulnerability. I understand the impulse, but I was determined to break the pattern. No matter how uncomfortable motherhood made me, the only running I planned to do was on the treadmill.

I sat down to take some of the pressure off my throbbing leg when my mom and Jason entered.

"What do you think?" my mom said, holding up the corner of her new teal bedspread. "I might have been too jazzed on Sudafed when I chose the color."

"Love it," I lied.

"It's maybe a little bright," Jason said, "but—"

My mom's face started to fall and I stopped Jason before he could finish.

"No, baby. It's perfect."

Like judging one of my mom's boyfriends as a kid, weighing in on her decorating was pointless and would only hurt her feelings. I found it easier to just smile and wait for things to change.

Later that night, I tucked Sid into his travel crib before collapsing on the teal bedspread I knew would be fuchsia by Christmas.

Jason rubbed my back, encouraging me to stay positive about the trip. He listed all of our favorite dive sites on the island and talked about how thrilled he was to test out his new scuba gear. I knew full well he'd probably end up impulse-buying some other shit he'd never use as soon as he wandered into the next dive shop.

For all my mixed feelings about my mother, I too was grateful to be in such a beautiful place, even if my bed didn't have a canopy.

I knew something was wrong when Sid started crying around 3 a.m. and I couldn't stand up to get him.

"Baby," I said to Jason, who was sound asleep next to me. "I can't put pressure on my leg. Something is wrong."

Jason flipped on the matching teal bedside lamp. "What do you mean?"

"I honestly don't know. It's too swollen to walk on."

Jason told me to stay put while he went to check on Sid. When he came back, Sid was in his arms with a hungry smirk on his face. He smacked his lips and latched onto me without opening his eyes. Jason, meanwhile, bent my leg up and down like a physical therapist.

"Does this hurt?"

"No," I said.

"How about this?" he asked, tapping on my patella.

"It's only when I stand," I explained tearily.

Jason waited for Sid to finish feeding, then changed his diaper and placed him back in his crib. Watching Sid float away in Jason's arms while I sat glued to the bed, I felt powerless and incompetent and like a human gas pump.

I woke up earlier than usual the next morning because of the time change. To my surprise, Sid and Jason were both still sleeping. I tested my leg and, sensing that it hadn't improved, I rolled off the bed and crawled on my hands and knees along the marble floor toward the bathroom.

Before I could get there, my mom stopped me.

"Chop? What are you doing?" She had a cup of coffee in one hand and Rocky in the other.

"My leg is really fucked up. I seriously can't walk on it."

My mom cocked her head at me like someone looking at a Sudoku puzzle for the first time.

"How are you gonna dive with one leg? I guess we can just throw you in and strap your tanks on once you're in the water."

Though I might have preferred a little concern, I had to admire her ability to make the best of a situation. She was always telling me to "buck up," to "get over it." When I was sick or injured as a child, she always found ways to keep the party going. She created portable ice headbands for dental work, started at-home IVs for menstrual cramps, and was never without a full prescription of Percocet. In some ways, the fact that my mom was a nurse was amazingly convenient. And in other ways, it was really fucking annoying. Having a parent in the medical field means never really getting any sympathy unless you're dying of AIDS. "Oh, your stomach hurts? Well, at least you aren't dying of AIDS." "You pulled a muscle in your groin? That sucks. But you know what sucks more? AIDS." This isn't to excuse her lack of empathy, but there is a certain desensitization that comes with seeing real illness on a daily basis. By comparison, my ailments were minor.

From my spot on the floor I heard Sid crying. Jason woke up to a half-empty bed, hyperventilating.

"Everything okay? Baby? Baby?" he called out, like he'd just dreamed I was mowed down by a school bus.

It didn't surprise me that I'd married a man who was the exact opposite of cavalier when it came to injuries. Jason was an overreactor of the highest degree. Not only was his threshold for pain low, but he was an actor. On countless occasions, he would take what I'd consider a small event and heighten it to a full-blown catastrophe. When he stubbed his toe, he'd start screaming like he was being sodomized with a hot poker.

"Oh MY GOD! FUUUUCK!" he'd howl, then do a Chaplin-esque pratfall and writhe on the ground in agony.

Sometimes I'd laugh at his act, but for the most part, I ignored him and charged ahead—the same way my mom was now doing with me. I never intended it to be hurtful. It just never occurred to me to make a big deal of it. He was *fine*. And he didn't have AIDS.

"Babe?!" he called again, then jumped out of bed and scrambled toward me.

"Yes?" I said, lying on my back now, staring up at my mom.

I explained to Jason that I was too afraid to stand on my leg for fear of damaging it further, but I needed to pee and hadn't wanted to wake him. I still needed to pee, but Sid was demanding he be removed from his crib and placed back on my boob. So Jason grabbed Sid while I climbed up my mom's body like a toddler and used her shoulder as a crutch to the toilet.

"This really blows," my mom said.

"Is there a doctor on the island who could look at me?" I sat on the toilet, defeated.

"Only on Maui."

Maui was a forty-five-minute boat ride away. The idea of packing up my leg and heading over to have some nurse practitioner give me an Ace bandage seemed like a giant waste of time. The other pitfall of having parents in the medical profession is that you become a know-it-all medicine snob. Whenever I needed a prescription my dad would write it for me. If I wanted to see a specialist I got right in. I was quick to throw around medical jargon: subcutaneous, anaphylaxis, hyperlipidemia. And aside from the one time I offered my high school boyfriend's father a Xanax instead of a Zantac, I was fairly adept. In many ways I feel like my entire life has been building to that one watershed moment where I get to storm through a crowd of concerned citizens and say, "Clear the way, people, I'm a doctor's daughter!"

From the bathroom my mom helped me outside to her new teak lawn chairs, where Sid was anxiously waiting. I nursed him and told Jason that I wanted to hold off on seeing a doctor. The plan instead was to head over to the hotel and ask for a pair of crutches.

Jason changed Sid's clothes and then obligingly changed mine.

"Chop-chop, Jen!" my mom called out from her personal golf cart, urgent, like an ambulance driver with a half-dead passenger in the backseat.

"I had the governor ripped out of this thing while we were in San Diego last month," she confessed as she peeled down the road toward the hotel.

"What's a governor?"

"You know, the brake that keeps you from hauling ass? Fuck that!"

She gunned it over a pothole just to prove her point. Sometimes I would look at her and wish I could be as cool. At her core she would always be that recalcitrant sixteen-year-old girl. The one who endured belt beatings from a brutal mother for sneaking out to see Led Zeppelin. The one who rode topless on the back of a Harley, protesting the war. For as much as she'd hurt me, my deepest desire was still to merge with her, to fully gain her acceptance and finally be let in. But like all the pretty, popular girls of grade schools past, she was always two steps ahead of me, with blonder hair and newer shoes, forever evading my grasp.

My mom parked her golf cart directly in front of the valet and told him not to touch it. She assured him she'd be right back; he naively believed her.

I sat in the cart with one leg propped up, staring at the sun-kissed surfer kid in his wrinkled polo shirt as my mom scampered into the lobby, looking for the hotel manager. I was used to my mom doing as she pleased, regardless of rules. One of the Moc's most notable quotes was "Rules don't apply to me," and for the most part, they seemed not to. She parked overnight in twenty-minute loading zones, cut airport security lines, and scored me a fake ID at fifteen so I could, as she put it, "continue hanging out with me." There was something so thrilling about being a part of her capers—being in on the con, even if it was just jockeying to get the best table at Nobu. Watching her in action was like watching James Bond walk into a party, tango his way into a backroom safe, steal a top-secret device, down three glasses of champagne, and then slip into an escape submarine off a nearby dock.

Fifteen minutes later, my mom popped back out of the lobby carrying a pair of crutches and a plate of pineapple that she'd probably taken straight off someone's table in the dining room. She offered the valet a piece that she expected him to eat out of her fingers (which he did), then got back in the cart and took off.

"All right, Choppy! We have crutches. They belong to Allen the Bartender, but he claims his ACL is pretty much healed, so you can borrow them for the week."

Bartenders loved my mom. She could drink like a Scotsman and was always able to persuade the table next to her to do a shot out of her navel. As long as you kept her fed and didn't pour tequila on her after midnight, she kept her clothes on and was a gift the whole family could enjoy.

When we got back to the condo I used Allen the Bartender's crutches to hop inside. I guessed that Allen was six feet tall, because every time I leaned on the crutches, my feet left the ground and I was suspended in the air like a gymnast on the parallel bars. I found a chair and Jason handed me Sid. He was smiling and warm from lounging in the sun.

"Do we think he's hungry again?" I said, searching for something I could offer him that Jason couldn't.

"I don't think so."

"Maybe he wants to take a nap?"

"No, he just woke up."

Sid started fussing and reaching for his toys on the floor. I placed him on the ground and propped up his back with a pillow.

"Choppy! Not that pillow, that's Rocky's."

I looked over to see Rocky fuming in the corner. He chewed on the same small toy he'd had since birth: the Baby Shoe. Rocky was obsessed with it and never let it out of his sight. Over the years, my mom had had to dismantle it and re-stuff it with a look-alike toy several times. I thought of the way my mom had discarded anything in the house that wasn't bolted down when I was a kid. This included my She-Ra: Princess of Power action figure, my Sweet Sea mermaid doll, and my cocker spaniel, Rusty.

Rocky and his baby shoe stayed back at the condo while the rest of us headed out to the beach. I tried getting the hang of my newly acquired crutches, but I kept tripping over my one good leg. Jason futzed with the crutches, attempting to lower them, but it was no use, they were too tall. I didn't want to stand (or *hang*, really) in the way of his scuba plans, so I urged him to get out on a boat and take a few dives. John disappeared to the golf course, and before I knew it, it was just me, my mom, and Sid.

I lost myself in the sterling-silver rings trapped around the Moc's overgrown toe knuckles, deformed from years of bar-hopping in python pumps. I watched as they repeatedly buried themselves in the sand, then reappeared like the crooked talons of a parrot, eternally perched on an invisible branch. I flashed to an image of her when she was young—so hopeful, so arrogant. I remembered the waves of flaxen hair that cascaded down her back, her ruffled string bikini, her acrylic French-manicured nails. I remembered how I would lie next to her on the beach for hours, longing for her to notice me, silently watching her skin bronze in the sun. When she wasn't home, she was out on a date. I'd find myself in her still-warm room with no expectation that I'd see her before bed. I'd sneak into her closet and try on her low-cut dresses. I painted myself with her Christian Dior lipstick, I drowned myself in her Calvin Klein Obsession eau de toilette. I wanted all of her and yet she kept me at such a distance. I fought off sleep, I fought off her suitors, anything to spend one more moment in her presence.

As I returned to the present, it dawned on me that with Jason gone, my mom was the only one I could rely on for assistance. I was bound to my beach chair. If Sid needed anything or, worse, if *I* needed anything, it was going to fall to her.

After ordering a beer and a coffee, my mom discreetly peeled back her top, exposing a dental floss–like bikini that barely hid her still-perfect breasts. I looked at her, both mortified and envious.

"What?" she asked, genuinely.

"Your boobs are basically out!"

"Not even! I usually catch rays topless. I'm just trying to be respectful of Sid. Nana is getting tan lines for you," she said to Sid as a cabana boy stood next to her, handing her both drinks.

"You know my boobs look this way only because I didn't

breast-feed you. It wasn't the cool thing to do back then," she informed the cabana boy as he walked off.

I'd been anticipating my mom's anti-breast-feeding rant for months.

"Formula saved my tits!" she called out proudly, adjusting her sunglasses.

"Did I ever latch on?"

"Oh, you tried, all the time! But I had to bat you away like you were a deranged little bird." She sipped on her beer and smiled, shedding light on why my nickname had been Bird before it was Choppy.

Eventually, Sid fell asleep under a makeshift chuppah between my legs. For the next four hours I listened to my mom rant about her three favorite topics: her condo in San Diego, how my sister's kids gave her pneumonia, and my dad's inability, after thirty-two years of divorce, to have a normal friendship.

"It's just, like, get over it already. What did I ever do to make things weird?" For as much as she protested, I think part of my mom loved the fact that she and my father still had an awkward dynamic. What annoyed me the most was that behind closed doors, things between them were amicable. It was only in front of us kids that my dad pretended he wanted nothing to do with her. He used her when it was beneficial, calling her up to ask for advice or to sniff out gossip. But when called out for yenta-ing, he would blatantly lie. My dad's ego was too big to admit to speaking to a woman who'd divorced him. And my mom's ego was too big to corroborate his lie, which constantly left them at an impasse.

We talked about my upcoming book release. Namely, the chapter about her.

"Oh, God! You don't talk about me having lots of boyfriends, do you? John won't like that!" she said, with faux modesty.

"Not really. Maybe? I don't know, it's supposed to be funny. Was I funny as a kid?" I asked, curious.

"Hmm . . . You might have been . . . I wasn't really listening." She looked out at the water as if she was genuinely trying to recall. "But I think you were pigeon-toed. That could be why your leg is fucked up. You know you are slightly pigeon-toed, right?"

When Jason returned he was salty, sated, and in completely different scuba gear than he'd left in. I tried to be happy for him and not guess how much money his new outfit cost.

"Did you have fun?" I asked, faking a smile.

"My dive watch was the wrong one. I gotta return it when we get home. But it's gorgeous out there. We saw two pods of spinner dolphins over at First Cathedral and the water is crystal clear," he said with the passion of a schoolboy who still thinks he's going to be a marine biologist. Jason grabbed Sid and we started packing up.

The longer I stayed off my leg, the more it seemed to hurt. I hurled my body toward my mom, forcing her to lend her support as I tried to stand.

"I can't keep using the crutches. They suck."

My mom suggested checking with the hotel for a wheelchair.

"Then at least you could hold Sid while we pushed you around," Jason said optimistically.

I wrongly assumed that after a day and a half of sitting, I'd be fully recovered. I wasn't. Not even remotely. In fact, I felt worse.

"I can't take this anymore. I need to get back to taking care of my child, not watching him fly in and out of my life like a set piece in *The Lion King*." The idea of cruising around the island in a wheelchair was maybe the only thing more embarrassing than sitting on the beach next to a scantily clad sixty-year-old whose tits had been suckled by everyone but me. The only other time I'd been in a wheelchair was when I was thirteen. My mom took a group of hemophiliacs to Disneyland and we ordered a handicap pass in order to skip the lines. None of the boys wanted to sit in the chair, so my mom made me do it. I'll never forget the looks of pity I got from worried strangers and park personnel. Little girls would whisper to their parents and point. Cute guys who under other circumstances might smile refused to acknowledge my existence. I was the Grendel of the entire theme park. But I agreed to explore the wheelchair option this time because Sid was more important than my image.

That evening, Jason and John took the golf cart back to the hotel while my mom helped me with Sid. The Moc sat on the bathroom counter, watching me float Sid around the bathtub. I tilted him backward and his hair splayed out like a fan around his face. He seemed happy and drowsy and blissfully unaware of the dysfunction with my leg and my mother. When I was finished, I lifted him out of the water for my mom to wrap him in a towel. My lack of mobility made asking for help less of an option than a necessity. Of the three people in the room, my mom was the only one on two working legs. It freed me from my own pride and inhibitions, because I didn't have to fear her rejection. She had no choice but to come through, and I secretly loved it.

After getting Sid to a safe place, my mom walked back over and helped me out of the tub without my even asking. Happily surprised, I nuzzled into her plush terry-cloth robe, still warm from the dryer, and tried to savor the sensation of her arms wrapped tightly around me.

"You got it from here, Choppy? Rocky's dinner has been in the oven for over an hour and he hates his meat overcooked." She angled me face-first toward the sink and let go.

I silently fumed. *How about instead of free-range chicken, Rocky makes himself a cream-cheese sandwich and waits for you to come home from a date that started two days ago?*

She gleefully scampered out of the room to the kitchen like a teenager whose boyfriend had come to visit her while she was babysitting. I looked at my adult self in the mirror, feeling foolish for my infantile thoughts. I couldn't let my frustration over my inability to take care of Sid take a backseat to my frustration over my mom's inability to care for me. But that was exactly what was happening.

An hour later, Jason and John arrived with Allen the Bartender's old wheelchair. It was roughly the same width as a Smart car.

"I guess that guy gets hurt a lot." John shrugged.

I'd been looking forward to feeling super-skinny in an oversize wheelchair, but this was a loveseat on wheels. I couldn't help but wonder if Allen needed a lap band.

The next morning, I sat patiently on my wheelchair bench as my mom pushed me around the hotel grounds. It was the closest I'd ever gotten to being pushed around in a stroller by my mom. She said she felt like they made her look like a hobo pushing a shopping cart, so she usually made one of her boyfriends carry me or just shoved me in her purse. Unlike with the crutches, I couldn't maneuver the wheelchair without her, and I didn't intend to try. I was a baby again in a giant fat-man stroller. I had my mom just where I wanted her: by my side, at my complete disposal.

I used the ramp to the restaurant, I used the largest stall in the lobby restroom, and I was crane-lifted into the swimming pool.

Sitting under an umbrella eating a spicy tuna roll, Jason covered his face with his hands as my mom worked the chair lift, lowering me into the deep end.

"I love you, baby," I called out, giving him nowhere to hide. I was starting to accept my disability and I wasn't going to let Jason distance himself from it. He was my husband and he made a vow to love me in sickness and in health, with legs and without.

Minutes after I was in the water, my mobility issues were eradicated. My limbs were lightened and I was free to move as I pleased. I swam laps up and down the crescent-shaped pool, weaving through pockets of day-drunk honeymooners and children learning to snorkel. I let out a small trickle of pee to test the water for that dye that apparently notifies the people around you that you are peeing on them.

"Looking good, Choppy!" my mom called out encouragingly. I glanced over my shoulder and saw my mom smiling. Her eyes were trained on me.

"Watch this!" I called back, dunking under and doing a handstand.

When I surfaced she wasn't watching. Instead, she was dangling Sid over the hot tub.

"Mom! What are you doing? He can't go in there!" I swam toward the adjoining Jacuzzi, draining my entire bladder along the way and demanding she pull Sid out.

"Jason?" I looked over at Jason, who'd been up with Sid all night and was now sleeping under his *National Geographic*.

"The pool is too cold for him," she said. "He likes this better because it's more like the womb."

"Mom, you can't put a baby in a hot tub," I said loudly, adjusting my voice as I heard the words coming out of my mouth.

"You can't? It's not that hot."

"I'm fairly certain you can't." I paused. I hadn't actually read anything about babies and hot tubs, but then again I hadn't really read anything about babies in general. "I'm almost positive."

"Excuse me, babies aren't supposed to be in Jacuzzis, are they?" I whispered to a passing pool boy.

"No. Definitely not." He looked at me, then at my mom, then at his manager, and walked away.

"Sorry, Sid. Your mom is being a total buzzkill." She rolled her eyes, pulling Sid up and taking him back to Jason. I tried to follow, but then remembered I still couldn't walk.

When my mom never returned to crane-lift me out of the pool, I decided that it was time to see a doctor. Something was drastically wrong, with my leg and my mother, and I needed to get a professional opinion on both.

"I can hang with Sid if you two wanna take the ferry over to Maui. I have a girl who could probably drive you to an urgent care, but I doubt you're gonna be able to get in for an MRI on such short notice." My mom ate what was left of Jason's sushi roll. Out of the corner of my eye, I could see a dollop of spicy tuna making its way toward Sid's virgin lips, but I intercepted it, smacking it away with my hand.

"Jason is half-asleep and doesn't know Maui at all. You need to take me."

"Me?" She was shocked by the idea.

"Yes. You *are* my mom," I reminded her.

"Then who's gonna watch Sid?" she said, confident she'd found a loophole in the plan.

"Sid has to come with us. I don't have enough pumped breast milk to leave him."

My mom's face dropped. She knew I had her trapped.

The Expedition Ferry slammed up and down as it cut across white-capped waves, fighting its way to Lahaina Harbor. Water splashed violently against the window as my mom looked out like a smoker stuck in after-school detention.

"Rocky is going to be so pissed he's missing his afternoon walk," she said with a groan. I could barely make out her bitching over the sound of the roaring engine under our feet. She'd complied with my wishes and come along for the ride, but like getting an overpriced lap dance, I was left feeling under-whelmed and more pathetic than before.

When we arrived in Lahaina, we met up with my mom's taxi-driver friend, Kiki. Kiki was an Asian woman who spoke in a super-loud high-pitched voice that sounded like a motor-

cycle sliding under a semi. She was nearly forty and six months
pregnant with her third child. Her maroon minivan taxi was
decked out in Mardi Gras beads, hula-girl dashboard bobble-
heads, and nori seaweed treats. A mix tape of nineties soft rock
played nonstop as we drove for an hour to the other side of the
island. Before leaving Lanai, I'd made an appointment with an
urgent-care clinic in Kahului that promised to give me an MRI
if my leg looked bad enough.

When we arrived at the clinic we made Kiki come in with
us and hold Sid. She rocked him back and forth as he stared at
her blankly, wondering if I'd given up on solo motherhood and
hired another baby nurse. My mom escorted me into an exam
room, where we waited for the doctor.

"How well do you know Kiki? Are you sure Sid is okay with
her?"

"She's the greatest. She's been driving me to the airport for
years," she said, as if being a great chauffeur somehow disqualified Kiki from being a kidnapper. I quieted my nerves by
reminding myself that Kiki already had two kids and one on
the way. She had her hands and her womb full. She knew better
than I did that stealing Sid would only bring more stress.

When a sun-damaged doctor walked in wearing a shark-
tooth necklace and a gold hoop earring, universal symbols of a
midlife crisis, I was dubious.

"Are you a real doctor?" I accidentally asked out loud.

"Ha! I think so," he said, then looked at my mom, who
seemed to be asking the same question with her eyes.

"So where is the MRI machine?" My mom squinted down
the hall like a suspicious DEA agent looking for a mountain
of dope.

"Yeah, we gotta take a look at this thing," I said, pointing at my leg.

"How did you injure it?" he asked, ignoring us and proceeding with his examination.

"Running."

He picked up my leg in almost the same way Jason did, tipping me off that he might not be a real doctor. My mom rolled her eyes and pointed at the time on her phone. I never felt closer to my mom than when we had a third person to hate.

"You don't have a break," he said, still playing with my leg.

"I know, but it's definitely something. I can't stand on it. Let's do an MRI."

"We actually don't have an MRI in this facility, and to be honest, it isn't going to show anything. Your best bet is just to go easy and let it heal itself."

I could already hear my mom's *I told you so.*

"So you're saying there's nothing to do?" I asked, annoyed.

"Nope. Not really. I think it's probably just tendinitis," he said, rushing us out, clearly eager to return to his life of surf, sun, and suing his ex-wife.

"So what does that mean? What do I need to do?"

"Walk on it, for starters."

"What?" I said, thinking I'd misheard him.

"Yeah, staying off it is only making it worse. The best thing you can do is start applying pressure and walking."

I looked at my mom. She looked back at me. I felt like a kid at the school nurse's office who just found out her temperature was just slightly below normal. What little concern my mom had faded as she walked out of the room behind me, pushing my empty wheelchair.

As we made our way back to Lahaina, Cher's "If I Could Turn Back Time" blasted through Kiki's low-fi speakers. The Moc had already moved on, buried in her phone and flashing me pictures of potential Murphy beds for her home office at each stoplight. I glanced at each picture with detached emotion, like an in-flight movie I didn't have the strength to turn off.

"I've always felt like John would be better suited to living in a man cave than sharing a room with me and Rocky," she mused aloud.

"Totally." I nodded, tuning out my mom and agreeing with Cher. I was too strong to tell her I was sorry (for dragging her to Maui), too proud to tell her I was wrong (about my leg), I knew that I was blind (at least more blind than paraplegic). And I started to realize that if I could turn back time, it wouldn't actually change a thing.

Days later, I boarded a flight bound for Los Angeles and real life. As we took off over Honolulu, I looked down at the serried sandy beaches and streets lined with rented Mustang convertibles. I mourned my injury and the self-awareness it forced on me. My leg wasn't broken, but a part of me was. More than fixing my leg, I guess I hoped that in Hawaii I could fix a relationship that had never functioned normally to begin with. I wanted my mom to *want* to take care of me. I wanted her to put me first. Before Rocky, before men, before herself. But looking to her for a corrective experience was futile and ill-timed. I needed to put Sid first. Before my own deprivation, before my beef with Rocky, before my morbid curiosity about

Allen the Bartender and whether or not he'd qualify for gastric. As the lights in the cabin dimmed and we were high above the clouds, I reclined my seat and quietly wept.

"Are you all right?" Jason panicked, sensing the irregularity in my breathing.

"I'm going to be." I smiled gently, reaching into Sid's diaper bag.

"Can I get you a tissue?"

"No, this is fine," I said, pulling out Rocky's Baby Shoe and nuzzling back into Jason's chest.

4
SLEEPING IN THE DOGHOUSE

When I was nine months pregnant, Jason decided it was the perfect time to buy a new house and uproot our life completely. He wasn't completely wrong—our home was in no way suitable for children. Our old place, though comfortable for a young couple or a drug dealer from the 1980s, dangled off the side of a cliff and was strictly filled with sharp objects and mirrored tables. He felt it made sense to move to a house that was more kid-friendly and less fun to do cocaine in.

It was July and Sid was five months old when we finally moved into our new place. He still wasn't sleeping through the night and his new favorite game was to wait until 2 a.m., then start screaming like he was being recircumcised. I'd made the mistake several weeks earlier of hanging over the side of his crib and dropping my boob into his mouth, feeding him like a hamster. Now he was under the impression that his milk was on tap and that Happy Hour was every hour.

So, one night, half-conscious, I got up and made my way

down the long narrow hallway to his nursery. When I entered, the room was pitch black. He continued screaming, my boobs inflating like airbags, getting bigger with each shriek. I picked him up and sat down in my rocking chair to feed him. The bathroom door was ajar, and for whatever reason I wanted it closed. Well—not *for whatever reason.* Open doors are unsettling. They promote tomfoolery among spirits and encourage home intruders to masturbate into your underwear drawers. I don't know how I know this. It's just information I was born with.

Jason stormed in, in one of his mother-hen frenzies, and fumbled around for no reason other than because he wanted me to know that he was awake, too. We were past the first stage of parenthood, in which we were generous with our time and happy to help each other out, and had now graduated to the second stage of parenthood, in which all we did was compete. If I got up at night, I shamed Jason if he didn't get up with me. If he changed a diaper, he was quick to let me know that it was by far the grossest diaper he'd ever seen.

I whispered to him to close the bathroom door. He did, then wandered around for a few seconds before returning to bed. Sid drank up like my mom at a bottomless-mimosa buffet, and an hour later, he was unconscious.

Slowly, I got up and tiptoed back to his crib, where I lowered him down on his side. Just then, something caught my eye. My reflection in the mirror. My reflection in the bathroom mirror.

The motherfucking bathroom door was open.

The air conditioner was off and the door was fifty pounds of oak, so it couldn't have opened from a stray draft. The alarm hadn't made a sound, so it couldn't be a break-in. As I saw it, there was only one reasonable explanation: ghost.

I tried to calm myself as I bolted out of the room and shut the door behind me. "Baby, can you come here for a second?" I called out down the hall.

Jason appeared a few minutes later, clearly having just been awakened but pretending he'd been up the whole time. I was standing with my back pressed against Sid's door, like a throng of hungry zombies were trying to break through from the other side.

"Yeah? Everything all good?"

His eyes were open and his mouth was moving, but he was still asleep. I amped up my volume to make sure I had his attention.

"Can you go in there and see if the bathroom door is open or closed?" I didn't want to hint at what the right response was, because husbands are trained to tell you whatever answer is most likely to shut you up. I also didn't warn him about the potential ghost, figuring that if I let it feast on his spirit for a while, it would give me and Sid more time to escape.

He opened the door, stumbled back into the room, flipped on a light, then walked back out. "It's open."

"What do you mean it's open?"

"I don't know. Maybe it's closed."

"No, it's not, Jason. It's open. You just checked. You gotta get Sid out of there. Can you please bring him to me?"

It dawned on me. *I had enclosed my only child in a room with an evil spirit for five full minutes.* This was what it was like to be a horrible parent. I was disgusted with myself and also, strangely, felt closer to my own parents.

"Bring him to you? He's asleep."

Jason started walking away, but I blocked him and pushed

his body through Sid's door, the way I planned on doing if the house was ever on fire. "BRING ME THE CHILD," I said.

Once my son was safe in my arms, I raced Jason back to the bedroom. Sid's mouth latched back onto my tit, and he hung off me like a giant clip-on earring, as my braless udders flapped. I checked around the room to make sure it was secure, then crawled under my duvet and switched my pillow to the opposite side of the bed.

"What are you doing?" Jason looked at me, confused, like someone who'd just lost a race across the house he didn't even know he was competing in. Mr. Teets trampled over my other two dogs, Gina and Harry, and curled up between my legs like a chastity belt (clearly dedicated to preventing me from being raped by Satan while I slept).

"I need to sleep on your side of the bed now. I'm scared of my side. It's too close to the door." I set Sid down on a pillow, which upon further reflection may have been Gina, and I burrowed in for the night.

Jason didn't have the strength to protest, or else he was unfamiliar with the fact that ghosts always eat the person closest to the door. Either way, he came to bed, closed his eyes, and fell asleep.

~

The next morning everything in the house looked different. I'd seen something I couldn't un-see. As a kid I used to always say aloud that I'd never want a ghost to reveal himself to me because I wouldn't be able to handle it and probably end up having a psychotic break. I figured announcing it to various rooms I found dubious was a great way to get my message across to the afterlife, without coming straight out and accusing any place in particular of harboring spirits.

"No need to reveal yourself, ghosts. My mom is fucking me up just fine on her own," I'd say casually while doing my homework.

Ironically, the only person I knew who'd ever actually seen a ghost was my mom.

"Well, Choppy, can't you just light some candles and make the place totally Jenny?"

"Totally Jenny? I don't even know what that means," I said into the phone. I paced back and forth on the patio as Jason stared at me passive-aggressively from the kitchen.

"I mean, get some sage and clear out the bad vibes."

"Mom, this is more than just bad vibes. I saw a ghost. Remember when you saw a ghost?"

"No. When?" My mom had this uncanny ability to block out all milestones in her life that others might deem notable: her college graduation, her first marriage, and now, apparently, all interactions with poltergeists.

I walked back inside, holding the phone to my ear with the kind of confidence that comes from knowing a ghost is going to kill you before brain cancer has a chance. "Mom, remember you told me you had a spirit attack you when we were house-sitting for your sister in Coronado?"

"I did?"

"What do you mean? How do you not remember that? You said it sat on your chest and held you down in bed and whispered that you had perfect, dime-sized nipples."

"It mentioned my dime-sized nipples? Maybe that sounds familiar. I don't know, I've blocked out a lot of my childhood."

"This was five years ago!"

While I was busy trying to explain to my mom that she was past middle age, Sid was busy head-butting Jason. I told my mom I'd call her back, even though I had zero plans to call her ever again, and hung up.

I took Sid from Jason so he could get ready for a meeting, then nonchalantly followed him around the house. Whatever room he walked into, I'd walk into. If he had to get something out of the dryer, I suddenly needed to start a load of laundry. If he had to make a second cup of coffee, I coincidentally needed to toast a piece of bread. He finally called me out when Sid and I appeared naked behind him in the shower and I suggested the three of us rinse off together as a family.

"Jenny, there is nothing wrong with the house. You are creating shit in your head. You need to get back on Zoloft."

One part of me believed him. The other part suspected that he'd promised Sid to another realm as a sacrifice in exchange for success in his acting career.

Get back on Zoloft? I thought to myself. *Was that what the neighbors drugged Mia Farrow with in* Rosemary's Baby? I was pretty sure it was.

Since my mom was a total dud in the ghost-busting department and Jason had officially adopted the role of "guy in the horror movie who doesn't believe in ghosts until one impales him with a harpoon in his sleep," I turned to my new replacement mom for advice.

Joan Arthur was a friend I'd made via Instagram a year and a half earlier. I knew who she was because we had all the same frenemies. She was a successful screenwriter with a reputation for telling networks that their notes made absolutely no sense. I remembered meeting her briefly years earlier when I auditioned for a pilot she wrote for ABC. I didn't get the job and didn't think of her again (except when hoping her pilot didn't get picked up) until I stumbled upon her Instagram. Unlike most of the accounts I followed, Joan's page told a story. Her voice was unmistakable and unique. She was narcissistic, unapologetic, hilarious, chaotic, and brutally honest. She was the kind of storyteller I aspired to be. Naturally, I found myself craving her friendship and approval. For a few weeks I followed her, hoping she'd follow back, but when she didn't, I grew offended, staged a screaming, dramatic breakup with her in my head, and deleted her ass. Then one day, a few months before I became pregnant with Sid, she texted me out of nowhere and said she'd heard I was funny. I didn't know how she got my number and I didn't care. She asked if I wanted to have dinner. Eager to win her over, I accepted.

That night I made my way up the long, treacherous staircase at the private, members-only Soho House in West Hollywood. After fighting my way through the line at the valet, I was confronted by the cunty sphinxes guarding the elevator.

"I'm meeting Ms. Arthur. She's expecting me," I said, hoping it might be that simple.

"There's no reservation under that name. Do you have another?" A tall brunette with two nostrils where her pre-Bat-

Mitzvahed nose used to be smiled down at me from a mahogany lectern.

I tried Joan's first name, my last name, then a random series of numbers, exclamation points, and ampersands until finally the sphinx beamed proudly.

"Found it," she said. "It was under Joan Arthur."

"I said that."

"You did?" She leaned back and feigned ignorance, overly confident in her kitten heels.

When I finally reached the rooftop garden, I was escorted to a table where a chic lesbian with an expensive, choppy blond haircut and mirrored Ray-Bans sat on a sofa, checking her phone.

"Honnnneeeeey," she said, as if reuniting with a long-lost lover. As she brushed her bangs to the side, I could see she was older than me, but her body looked roughly fourteen. She threw her phone at her Balenciaga motorcycle bag and started talking.

"The food is horrible here, but I love the ambience. You're not really into food, are you?" She picked a piece of focaccia out of the bread basket and sniffed it. "Feel my abs. I was a swimmer and I never had children." I dutifully touched her abs. They were rock hard, like a loaf of French bread that had been left out overnight. "You're not planning on having children, are you, honey? It'd be kind of pointless to become friends with you if you are. People with infants make the worst friends."

"I . . . Not anytime soon," I said with confidence.

Three months later, I was pregnant. Joan wasn't thrilled with the idea of me turning into a real-life Russian doll, but she accepted it so long as there was only ever going to be one mini-doll inside me. "You aren't going to have more than one kid, are you, honey? One is kind of chic but two is a fucking nightmare," she texted me. I imagined she was speeding down Sunset Boulevard in her black Mercedes G wagon with bullet-proofed windows.

"Of course not," I lied.

After that first foodless dinner, where we bonded over being left-handed Geminis with boozy mothers, Joan and I were spiritually inseparable. No matter how many babushkas popped out of me, I knew Joan wasn't going anywhere. We texted and spoke on the phone eight times a day, sometimes saying little more than "Honnnnnneeeeey" and then hanging up. The other players in my life were jealous at first and probably even a little threatened, but, like all my obsessions, they assumed this one would pass. It didn't. Joan was the kind of woman I'd been looking for all my life. In her, I found not only a friend but a mentor. She looked after me. She remembered dates of things. She sent flowers and wrote cards. She threatened to kill people who didn't help my career. She was the mother I always wanted—only better, because unlike my real mother, I was never going to lose her to a man.

If my real mom wasn't willing to indulge my haunted-house notions, I knew Joan Arthur would.

"And finally, *this* is the room that I think it lives in," I said, slowly leading Joan into Sid's nursery bathroom.

"Hmm . . . Honey?" Joan walked up to the antique mirror hanging above the sink and stared into it.

"Yeah?" I replied, worried she was going to ask if I also saw a young Gold Rush widow in mourning attire staring back at us.

"Do you think I look like Garth from *Wayne's World*?" Joan teased her bangs in the mirror and cocked her head to the side. "I think I might need to grow out my hair because people are commenting on all my photos that I look like him."

Joan's vanity didn't faze me. I'm the daughter of a man who asked for head shots for his birthday; if anything, it felt like home. In that moment, actually, it came as a great relief. If Joan felt comfortable enough in my haunted bathroom to fixate on her hair, there probably weren't any ghosts trying to use my mirror as a portal to hell. Soothed, I bid her farewell and we didn't speak again until five minutes later.

"So I never even asked what your feelings were about the house," I said, sitting at my computer and avoiding writing by googling pictures of myself with dark hair.

"Oh. It's definitely haunted," Joan said. "I couldn't wait to get out of there."

"What?" I slammed the keyboard.

"Medium Coke," she replied.

"Are you talking to me?"

"No, girl, I'm at McDonald's."

"Can you refocus? What about the ghost? Do I really have one?"

"Yeah, honey. I smelled him as soon as I walked in," she said nonchalantly.

"Him?" I asked, looking around the room, panicked.

"I've always had a nose for ghosts. I had this angry queen living in my Studio City house. Think he was a writer on some Aaron Spelling show. Clearly threatened. He used to try to break my Emmys while I was sleeping."

"I cannot believe you left me in my house alone when you knew there was a ghost," I wailed. I was hurt. I was also disappointed in myself for fusing with yet another nonmaternal mother.

"Honey, he's a friendly ghost, he's Jewish."

Unappeased, I hung up and ran out of the house. I called Jason and told him that Joan confirmed the ghost and that we needed to get in touch with our realtor immediately.

" 'Confirmed the ghost'?" Jason's voice hit an octave I'd heard only once, on our honeymoon, when I bit the tip of his penis as a joke.

I covered my mouth with my hand as I spoke so as not to make the ghost aware of my plans. "Baby. Why are you already so wound up? We just need to relist the house and move back into our old place."

Due to its unique specifications—namely, a driveway that looked like an X Games half-pipe—our old house was still sitting dormant on the market. If I moved swiftly, I could be packed up and back in it by the weekend.

"YOLO," I declared proudly.

"I'm gonna kill Joan," Jason mumbled. "This isn't like an undisclosed mold problem or something. If you call the realtor, he's gonna think you're nuts."

"He already thinks I'm nuts." I reminded Jason of how I refused to go into escrow until I camped out at our new home overnight to make sure it didn't feel like the scene of the

Tate/LaBianca murders. Standing outside and looking around the pool, I was now pretty certain it looked EXACTLY like the scene of the Tate/LaBianca murders.

"Yes, and you said you felt fine."

"That's because I was pregnant and full of hormones. Now my womb is empty and I'm back to operating from a place of constant fear and distrust." I walked back inside into the living room to make sure my housekeeper Lita wasn't shaking Sid uncontrollably.

"We aren't moving." He hung up.

I was embarrassed as I explained to Lita why I needed her to sit with me in the bathroom while I washed my hair.

"You don't sense anything?" I asked, shampoo in my eyes.

"No." Lita bounced Sid up and down on her lap while sitting on the toilet and trying to avoid staring at the stream of breast milk trailing down my chest.

It was a Tuesday and I was already running late for our Mommy and Me class in Santa Monica. I was excited to get Sid out of the house, but more excited to get myself out of the house. Sid didn't seem too bothered by the ghost, which meant one of two things: the spirit was benevolent or his soul had already been captured and I was living with a demon seed.

I felt bad about leaving Lita alone in the house, but not bad enough to interfere with my skinny jeans getting washed. I told her to take her time with the laundry, but to feel no obligation to finish the dishes if they started flying around the kitchen.

Baby's First Session in Santa Monica was one of those super-obnoxious classes you had to sign up for a year before you even planned on being pregnant, so obviously I had to rely on my sister's connections to get me in at the last minute.

"If you don't know somebody, you might get in, but you'd never get in with Abby. And if you don't get in with Abby, you might as well kill yourself," she'd said. My sister was never one to mince words.

Apparently there was another Mommy and Me class in the Valley, but if you told people you were in the Valley class, they assumed you were over forty, single, and a casting director.

I agreed to take the Santa Monica class mainly because I felt pressured by society to do so. In the past, I'd never been one to cave to convention, but that was before I had someone I really needed to impress: Sid. I knew he wouldn't remember it one way or the other (until he was old enough for my sister to get him alone and give a detailed account of all my shortcomings), but I wanted to be perfect for him. And according to my peers and strangers I followed on Instagram, being perfect meant socializing with other moms and babies.

I pounded the intercom to get in the locked glass doors of Saint Vincent's east wing. The introductory e-mail probably included a code I was supposed to memorize, but I don't read e-mails with the words "Mommy," "Group activity," or "Children" in the subject. After sneaking in behind a more responsible parent, Sid and I made our way to the third-floor classroom.

Class had already started. I unbuckled Sid from his stroller, took my shoes off, and tiptoed in. The class turned and looked at me like I was Satan. I double-checked Sid's forehead to make sure there wasn't an emblazoned *666*. I then placed him in the circle next to a little girl wearing a Missoni turban. Eight women between the ages of thirty and thirty-five sat cross-legged on the spongy, checkered floor. Some breast-fed and bitched about their bodies. Some bragged about their kids sleeping through the night. One mom that I found particularly fucking irritating was this blond chick, Mirial, who translated everything anyone said into sign language. All of the babies were under six months old, even though two looked like middle-aged Jewish accountants. I was pretty sure none of them understood sign language.

"Does anyone else have any concerns they want to discuss before we sing our goodbye song?" Abby, our instructor, asked.

Apparently, class started at ten-fifteen, not eleven-fifteen as I'd thought. Abby looked over at me and faintly smiled, as if my sister had already warned her I was a total flake. "Let's go to Starbucks and have our own class," I whispered to Sid, who was getting his imaginary taxes done by one of the accountants.

Before the singing could commence, Mirial, the annoying blonde, started desperately rambling, as if once class was over she was going to be thrown back into solitary confinement until her husband came home from work and beat her over the head with his dick. "Hi, guys, Mirial again." She signed her name twice, as if she was waiting for us to mirror it back to her. "Anyway, my 'area' has just been so sore since having little Jagger. I'm so tight, my husband can barely fit inside me." The only thing I found more annoying than a mom who unnecessarily uses sign language was a mom who pretended to still care about sex.

Abby explained that her estrogen levels were low because of breast-feeding. She recommended a cream.

"Does anybody in here have a ghost problem?" I said. I

looked at Sid, worried he might start shrieking like a vampire at the mere mention of the word.

"You mean like a phantom pain?" Abby replied.

"No, more like a literal phantom. Not *of the Opera,* more *of the underworld.*"

The room went silent. Mirial's signing fingers twisted into horns on her head. The accountants started crying.

Class was dismissed on that note. As I tried to strap Sid's flailing body back into his stroller, Abby walked up behind me and tapped me on the shoulder. She was an extremely petite woman with pale skin and a neck full of birthstone charms.

"I didn't want to say this in front of the group, but I do believe in ghosts and I have a great psychic who specializes in this kind of thing, if you'd like to speak with her." She told me she'd text me her clairvoyant's number and not to worry.

Before I exited the building, I rolled past a small marble fountain and sprinkled what I assumed was holy water on Sid's face. He didn't burst into flames, but he also didn't look happy. I tried to lighten things up on the drive home by playing "Head, Shoulders, Knees, and Toes" on the stereo on repeat. Every stoplight, I'd look in the rearview mirror to check if he was awake. He was always awake. Part of me wondered if he might be one of those people who slept with their eyes open. The other part suspected he was an incubus.

It's a strange feeling to both love and fear something in equal parts. I didn't know if I made him happy. He couldn't tell me. I didn't know if he wanted to kill me. He was strapped in a car seat. All I knew was that I loved him violently—to the point of madness. But the intimate serenity of pregnancy, that weightlessness that can be replicated only by a muscle relaxer and a tall glass of wine, had vanished and in its place grew a thundering, inexorable terror.

Just as I pulled up to our well-appointed albeit demonic home, Sid fell asleep. I scanned the upstairs windows of the house, sure I'd see the kid from *The Omen* peering out through one of the curtains, but everything looked calm. Lita's car was gone. She usually worked later, but knowing there was a greater chance of her being deported than apported, I tried not to read into it. I parked and waited for Jason rather than disturb Sid.

I looked around at the lush greenery cascading off the hillside. I watched the sunlight cut through the fanning palms above. I scanned for unmarked Indian burials. I told myself that I should be happy, that everything was good. But not even the half-eaten Quest Bar in my glove box could suppress my pangs of discomfort.

I looked at my phone and found a text from Abby. Her psychic's name was Elenor. I called right away.

"Hi, my name is Jenny Mollen, er . . . Biggs, and—" Before I could finish leaving a message, my other line beeped.

I clicked over and it was Elenor.

Her voice was soft and sympathetic and slightly less "Come to the light, Carol Anne" than I'd anticipated. Part of me wanted to hang up before she told me anything that might make me check into a hotel; the other part waited with bated breath for the gory details.

Torn between what I wanted and what I needed, I blurted out, "Do you think my house is haunted because I totally think it's haunted oh my God I'm scared."

There was a long pause on the other end of the phone, followed by what sounded like a cockatiel being shoved into a microwave. Finally, Elenor spoke.

"It's a little haunted."

"A little haunted? What does that mean? How can something be a little haunted? Is it haunted by a little person?" I looked at Sid in the backseat and flashed to the little boy who kills his mother in *Pet Sematary*.

"I think the spirit is actually a large dog."

"A dog?" I exhaled for the first time in two minutes. I knew that dogs, unlike people, were inherently good.

"Yes."

Now that I thought about it, a dog ghost made a lot of sense. Ever since we moved in, Harry and Teets had been marking the walls incessantly. What I thought was just a simple game of dueling penises was probably a concerted effort to establish dominance over the former tenant. Having a ghost dog seemed kind of fun. Jason always wanted to adopt a bullmastiff or a standard poodle, but we traveled too much and didn't have the space in the old house. Maybe a large ghost dog was exactly what we needed. Husky, low maintenance, omnipresent.

"Like a Clifford the Big Red Dog? That's how I'm picturing him. Because I have three small dogs and none of them are strong enough to open bathroom doors."

"He's more the size of a cocker spaniel."

"Teets hates cocker spaniels," I said, hoping to at least steer her toward a bichon frise.

"Oh, and he has an old-man partner." Elenor's microwave beeped. No sound from the cockatiel. "Somebody who lived near the property. He's going to teach your son historical facts."

I envisioned a man in a tricornered hat floating over Sid's crib, quizzing him about the signatories of the Declaration of Independence. Now I wasn't just scared of the ghost, I was a little bit offended. Had the universe assigned me this apparition because it assumed I'd be a shitty history teacher? Would Sid also be visited by ghosts tutoring him on other topics I was deficient in, such as industrial arts and arithmetic?

I moved the baby monitor to Jason's new side of the bed (my old side) to ensure I wouldn't see any floating old-man hands swipe through the frame when I least expected it. The monitor was always wherever Jason was, because even before I had confirmation of a ghost, baby monitors scared the shit out of me. Like all surveillance cameras, if you watch them long enough, something usually levitates. The room felt colder than normal, a sure sign that we weren't alone.

"Who do we know with a midsize dog that was recently murdered?" I asked, crawling into bed next to Jason. I'd read online earlier that the number one reason a ghost haunts a place is because it doesn't know it's dead. "What was the name of Jerry and Mike's Lhasa apso?"

A guy at Jason's gym had accidentally killed his six-year-old dog two months earlier. The dog had sneaked into the backseat of his car one morning before work and was found "sleeping" on the dashboard later that afternoon.

"Jenny! NEVER MENTION THAT EVER. I'm serious. That was the most devastating thing that ever happened to

Jerry. And the dog was a Pekingese. Seymour, I think." Jason paused, contemplating the name.

"Seeeeymour?" I called out, dangling my head off the end of the bed and looking under it.

Jason looked at me, incredulous. "Jenny, you are an adult. I need you to act like an adult. Ghosts aren't real. This is our home. You need to stop being afraid of it."

The notion sounded so simple. And I wished deeply that I could. I didn't want to be afraid of my new house. I didn't want to be afraid of my new life. But I was. Desperately and utterly afraid.

Everywhere I went for the next month I found myself talking about the ghost. Business meetings, television pitches, the dog groomer. I bought a three-pack of sage smudge sticks from Whole Foods and walked through each room making smoke triangles. I opened all the windows and doors and chanted the words "If you are not of this realm, you need to leave." I even made Lita spend the night in Sid's room to see if anything would happen to her. I was sleeping less as Sid was sleeping more. I knew something had to change.

My therapist, Chandra, whom I'd recently sent Joan Arthur to for a full psych eval, suggested that I might be projecting other woes onto the house. I agreed that it was possible. But what was equally possible was that the ghost was reaching out to me because it had unfinished business in this lifetime.

One afternoon, Jason took Sid to the park and I sat in the front yard doing a phone session with Chandra. I preferred phone sessions because Chandra's office was on the other side of town and because if I got bored of whatever she was talking about I could look at Twitter. Teets sat on my lap, tuning out, as Gina and Harry scavenged around for pieces of petrified deer poop.

"Maybe I'm like Whoopi Goldberg—" I started to say, just as the other line beeped and I took it. It was Elenor the Psychic. I told her I'd call her back for counsel just as soon as I hung up with my therapist. I didn't tell her when that would be; I assumed she knew.

Twenty-five minutes later I called. "Okay," I said, "Chandra thinks this entire situation is a case of classic projection." I waited for Elenor to weigh in.

"Fear manifests in different ways, Jenny," she said after a moment. "Maybe it isn't about a house or a ghost or anything other than your real fear of being a parent."

I looked at my phone to make sure I'd actually hung up with Chandra. She and Elenor were starting to sound a lot alike. Both were trying to steer me toward rational explanations for my totally irrational fears. It was infuriating.

I grabbed the conversational wheel and turned us back into the weeds, where it was safe. "The truth is I'm fine with the dog. I'm just sort of taking issue with this old-man partner. Is there a way to split them up?" I started fantasizing about a three-way call with Elenor and Chandra. One three-way phone call with my therapist and my psychic might literally solve my entire life.

"You can't escape your own psychological demons, Jenny. You need to ask yourself what you're really afraid of before you just up and move."

"You think they might be *demons*?" I wanted to probe further, but Joan Arthur and my realtor, Eric Kessleman, were ringing at the front gate. I hung up.

I could see only the bottom half of Joan's body as I approached. The rest of her was obscured by the avocado tree straddling our property line as she attempted to scale the fence.

"I think you guys changed the code!" Eric shouted as one of Joan's Marni boots kicked him in the head.

I punched a code in my phone and the gate opened, pulling Joan's body out of the tree. Joan wrapped her heels around the gate and rode in like a rodeo cowboy. I walked down the driveway to meet them and Eric held his hands out to help Joan down.

"Yeah, honey, that was fairly easy to climb and I'm fifty-four-ty." She glanced at Eric. "Imagine if I was a strapping young black guy with an erection! Good thing you're selling." Joan pulled up her slim-fitting cargo pants, then wiped her hands on my back while pretending to give me a hug. "Does anybody have hand sanitizer?"

I'd explained to Eric that I might want to relist the house, but I didn't get into details over the phone. I thought it'd be best to wait until we were face-to-face to mention supernatural activity.

Eric was a handsome gay man in his midforties. He always wore a jacket with an open-collar shirt and small, studious spectacles. He drove a sensible car, said sensible things—I trusted Eric. He seemed like the kind of person who had his life figured out—the kind of guy who read Eckhart Tolle and did Self-Compassion workshops at Esalen. I'd never been to Eric's house, but I pictured it smelling like sandalwood and spa water. Eric wasn't the type of guy who'd ever be called on to do the bidding of a ghost dog and his old-man partner.

"I just basically wanted you to see the changes we've made

and tell me if you think we could get our money out. PS, Jason has no idea you're here and we can't tell him." I led Eric past the pool to the front door.

Joan turned to him and said all the things I didn't have the courage to. "It's haunted, girl," she said in a foreboding tone. Joan called everyone "girl," regardless of gender. "Ghost dog. Old-man partner."

"I see." Eric remained calm as he looked up at the wood-beamed ceiling. "Opening up the kitchen made a huge difference," he offered.

As upbeat as Eric tried to be, I sensed his underlying disappointment. He took pride in his work. If his clients weren't happy, neither was he. And his clients here weren't happy. Well, one of the clients, anyway. The other client had absolutely no idea any of this was happening.

I rattled off a list of improvements we'd made to the Spanish Colonial Revival as we made our way down the long hallway toward the nursery. The outdoor pizza oven, the built-in Miele coffee machine, the fifteen hidden security cams, the biometric keyless deadbolts on all the doors and windows.

"The foodie and the freak. That's my nickname for them." Joan picked up one of Sid's jackets sitting on a club chair and tried to put it on.

"Jason wanted to install a Toto toilet and I wanted a moat and drawbridge, but we're both unemployed at the moment, so we thought we should hold off."

I flung open the door to the nursery, hoping to catch the old-man partner carving a corncob pipe in my glider, to no avail.

"Honey, this basically fits me!" Joan said, sausaging herself into Sid's jacket.

Eric wasn't sure what to think. He admitted it would be hard to make a profit on the place so quickly, then guesstimated that if we held the house for another year we'd most likely break even.

"A year? I'll be dead in a year! What about all those people who flip houses? I kind of thought that's what I did here."

Eric explained that the pizza oven, though a great perk, didn't add any square footage to the home.

"You could always just bulldoze and rebuild something massive and fabulous." Joan never offered a solution that cost less than a million dollars.

"Or we could move you back into your old place and you could rent this out—" Before Eric could finish, Jason stormed through the front door with Sid.

I looked at the owl clock perched on Sid's bookshelf. They were home early. If Jason caught me with Joan Arthur and our realtor in Sid's bedroom, I was busted. If Eric Kessleman was given the opportunity to talk to Jason before he was properly primed, the deal would be off.

The floor creaked as Jason marched down the hall.

"Babe?" he called out.

With no way out, I scrambled to hide Eric and Joan. I flung open the French doors on Sid's creepy closet and shoved Eric in. "Just wait here," I whispered eagerly, "and I'll come get you once the coast is clear."

Joan followed and sat on his lap. "You don't mind if I sit on you, do you, girl? I'm kind of bony," she said proudly. Closing the doors in their faces, I promised to return as quickly as I could.

After scanning the room to make sure everything looked normal, I shut out the lights and turned to go.

Just then, Jason appeared. He was holding Sid, who had spit up all down his Nirvana onesie. Jason gave me an awkward kiss on the chin, then brushed past me to change Sid's clothes.

"Feel my abs," I heard the closet whisper as I walked over to help.

"What?" Jason said, distracted.

"Nothing, baby. How was the park?" I said loudly.

"Good, aside from Sid vomiting all over the car. I'm such an idiot! I shouldn't have given him a bottle before the ride home." Jason shamed himself out of habit. I'd grown to hate it when he called himself names or beat himself up. Jason was no longer just Jason to me. He had been a little boy once. A little boy who needed to be perfect, who never got the unconditional love that our child would. I wished I could go back and save him. I wished I could go back and save myself.

Holding Sid by one leg and grabbing a new diaper with his free hand, Jason glanced at me and smiled.

"I'm impressed you're all alone in the nursery. This is huge progress."

I smiled and offered to take over, but he refused. My boobs were engorged and ready for release, but Sid had just eaten.

"You go pump. I'll put him down for a nap," he said sweetly.

What the fuck was I supposed to do? Jason was being so helpful. He was the guy I wanted him to be at two in the morning. If I argued, I'd be negating all the complaining I'd done for the last two months. If I didn't, Joan and Eric would be stuck in the closet for the next hour.

Weighing the pros and cons of each scenario, I decided that healthy co-parenting meant more to me than Eric Kessleman's comfort. So I left the nursery and returned to the bedroom to watch patiently on the monitor. Jason rocked Sid in his arms and danced lightly around the room. My pulse raced; I prayed Joan would sit still and wait for my return. Sid looked up at the ceiling, probably learning about the battle at Yorktown, when suddenly there was a sound.

"Honnnnney?" the closet whispered.

Jason turned and looked directly at the closet. It didn't move. Curious, he walked closer.

"Girl?" the closet inquired.

Jason looked confused. We were new parents. We were tired. Was his mind playing tricks on him? Still holding Sid, he reached toward the French doors and tried to pry them open. They wouldn't budge. Maybe he'd baby-proofed them on the wrong side. I called to him from the bedroom, hoping to distract him.

"Baby? Everything okay in there?"

"I'm fine," he called back.

To my great surprise, Jason suddenly stopped futzing with the doors and laid Sid in his crib. I was both relieved and horrified. How many other times in our marriage did he think he'd heard something and then completely brushed it off? I could be dead and maimed in a bathtub filled with my own blood and Jason probably wouldn't notice until he decided to use the neighboring shower and there was nobody there to hand him a towel.

Once Sid was down, Jason directed his attention back toward the closet. I dropped the monitor and ran back down the hall to stop him, but just as I opened the nursery door, he opened the closet. Jason screamed. Eric screamed. Sid broke into hysterics. And Joan sat completely still, as if Sid's baby coat provided her with camouflage.

It took Jason weeks to forgive me for almost selling our new house out from under him. But with couple's therapy and several halfhearted blowjobs, we reached an understanding.

It occurred to me a few weeks later, as I sat with Jason and Sid in the American Airlines lounge waiting to board a flight to New York, that I might not have the kind of ghosts I could leave behind by moving, but the kind that rent space inside my head. Maybe it was easier to say I was afraid of the house than to admit I was afraid of being a mom. I didn't want to obsess over intruders or whether I was going to be a good enough teacher for my son. I didn't want to be the outcast of my Mommy and Me group or the lady who makes her housekeeper watch her shower. I didn't want to be guided by my fear. I wanted to be the kind of mom who hears a weird noise in her front yard, walks outside with nothing but her bare hands, and returns wearing a raccoon bolero.

I needed Sid to trust me. I needed to trust myself.

So for the time being I agreed to stay in the new house.

The lounge started to clear out when a voice came over the loudspeaker announcing boarding. Jason quickly ran to the bathroom as I packed up our carry-ons and prayed Sid's Benadryl was kicking in. Out of nowhere, a hand touched my shoulder. I turned to see Jerry, Jason's friend from the gym.

He wore a baseball cap that covered his insanely curly hair and a cashmere tracksuit that screamed "My other tracksuit is even more cashmere than this tracksuit."

"Hey, you. Haven't met the little guy yet, but I've seen tons of pics." Jerry reached out to pet Sid on the head the way I imagined he used to pet Seymour, his late Pekingese.

"How is it going?" I asked in a sympathetic tone that implied I already knew he'd accidentally murdered his dog.

"You know. It's been hard. Mike didn't eat for two weeks. Every time we walk past the dog park I break into hysterics." Jerry teared up as he listed the holes Seymour had left in his life.

I couldn't help thinking this run-in wasn't a coincidence but some sort of divine intervention. I knew Jason said never to mention Seymour to Jerry, but maybe Seymour *needed* me to mention Seymour to Jerry. If I wanted to seize the moment and gain favor with my ghost dog and his old-man partner, I needed to act fast.

Out of the corner of my eye I saw Jason walking briskly back from the bathroom. He flapped his wet hands in the air as he made a beeline for us. My moment was about to pass.

"Let's have dinner when you guys get back from New York." Jerry picked up his backpack and purple titanium roller bag to leave.

I pictured our dinner ending in Seymour using my body to kiss Jerry on the mouth, like he was Demi Moore in *Ghost*.

"Jerry." I grabbed his wrist and stared into his eyes. Jason appeared next to me, but it was too late, the words kept coming out. "This might sound crazy, but . . . Seymour wants you to know that he forgives you."

Jerry's face lost all color and I thought for a moment he might faint.

Jason looked at me, mortified. I could almost see him tallying up the blowjobs I'd owe him. So far, his count was up to infinity.

Jerry pulled out a pair of sunglasses and used them to conceal the tears. He leaned over to my ear and whispered: "Thank you."

"You're welcome," I said loudly, as I looked at Jason and smiled like I was the Long Island Medium. "Oh, and one more thing, Jerry. Was there anyone else in your car that day? Maybe an old man?"

5

ATLAS RUGGED

Aman's midlife crisis starts with him buying a sports car. A woman's midlife crisis starts with her calling herself an interior decorator. After talking about it in couple's therapy, Jason and I decided we'd try to live in our ghost house for a year before making any rash moves. Our therapist, Beth, encouraged me to take whatever measures I needed to make myself feel comfortable in the new space.

That meant decorating. After all, I wasn't living in a midcentury-modern fuckpad anymore. I was living in a tile-roofed hacienda with absolutely zero fucking. I needed décor that complemented my new architecture and celibacy. I saw myself surrounded by African mud cloth and Indian block printing. I wanted miles of Thai batik runners and heavy Bolivian blankets, called *frazadas,* that I'd throw over my bed. I wanted to buy baskets from Botswana and fill them with firewood that I'd never burn. My house would be an eclectic clash of cultures that at best made me look like a seasoned editor for

Condé Nast Traveler, and at worst like an eccentric retired theater professor who collects tribal masks.

I began by scouring countless Pinterest pages for inspiration before realizing I was missing a key element: *I needed a Moroccan rug.* They were everywhere. Whenever I'd look up somebody fashionable on Instagram that I envied too much to actually follow, I'd inevitably scroll down and see a picture of their latest handbag strategically shot at a high angle on the same cream pile-weave rug with a black trellislike pattern woven throughout. These weren't just any Moroccan rugs; they were Beni Ourains. Beni Ourains hail from the eastern Middle Atlas Mountains of Morocco and are traditionally used as blankets to protect from the cold. Each rug is one of a kind because the weavers intentionally weave inaccuracies into their work to ward off the "evil eye." Objectively, these rugs are fairly basic, but like any trend (read: Birkenstocks), if you see it enough times you eventually become convinced you cannot live your life without it.

A bit of research told me that an authentic eleven-by-fourteen Beni Ourain rug could cost me as much as $20,000. I wanted one so badly I was tempted to visit ABC Home and order one on the spot. But I had a kid and an unpredictable menstrual cycle, and was unwilling to spend more than $5,000 on anything that was cream. So I did some browsing.

I started out talking to an Etsy seller named Mustapha. I knew that Etsy allowed for negotiation, so I was careful to conceal my identity and appear as though I had a deep understanding of what I was talking about. I wasn't a postpartum-battling ghost whisperer. I was Bertrand, the bi-curious interior designer with a penchant for travel. On one of my pillow-buying binges I'd discovered that most online vendors offer a discount to industry professionals. As Bertrand, Mustapha would know better than to take advantage of me. Bertrand was worldly, after all. He had expensive taste and was used to getting his way. If Mustapha couldn't provide Bertrand with what he was looking for at the price he demanded, Betrand would have no problem going elsewhere.

I reached out about an eleven-by-fourteen and he promptly replied. In broken English, he proposed a price of $6,800. "Do you design homes?" he added.

Here was my opportunity to let my expertise shine. Yes, I'm a designer, I told him. I explained that I lived in Los Angeles with my on-again, off-again lover, Trevor, and my golden doodle, Catherine Zeta Bones, but that I traveled extensively for work. I told him $6,800 was far too much. Bertrand knew better than to settle on a first offer. He might even travel to the source and pick something out himself, if that's what it took.

Mustapha strongly urged me against visiting Morocco. "Morocco is very difficult place to be," he said. "Crazy strange lions that eat everyone. They share food and shelter with the humans."

Lions that eat everyone? What the fuck was he talking about? Was Mustapha really trying to dissuade me from traveling to Morocco with the threat of lions? I felt lied to and manipulated. Bertrand would never stand for that. Without hesitation, I promptly ghosted Mustapha and moved on.

After a couple more days of Web surfing, I stumbled on a blog post on Apartment Therapy introducing me to The Anou. The Anou was a community of artisans, including women weavers, living in the Ait Bouguemez valley of the High Atlas Mountains. In 2010, Dan Driscoll, a guy from San Diego, was serving in the Peace Corps in the neighboring Moroccan region of Azilal. He was horrified when he learned that the weavers he met were practically penniless, even after selling their high-end tapestries to fair-trade organizations. Dan decided the solution would be to help build a website where the community could reach consumers without going through middlemen. And thus The Anou was born.

I inquired and learned that for $1,600, The Anou would weave me an eleven-by-fourteen Beni Ourain and send it to me in L.A. with no additional shipping costs. The rugs were beautiful, but unless they were being mass-produced in Indian sweatshops, I didn't understand how they could cost so little. So, before placing an order, I sent Dan an e-mail explaining what I wanted and double-checking that he wasn't a slave trader. Dan responded instantly. He defended the integrity of his operation and told me not to hesitate in calling him if I had any further questions.

Dan seemed like the kind of guy who regularly used every feature on his Swiss Army knife. He probably knew how to tie at least three hundred different kinds of knots. He could kill a Moroccan street lion with his bare hands. He was proficient and competent in all the areas I wasn't. I pictured him extracting his daily water from a cactus, sleeping in a Bedouin hut, and telling me he wished I wasn't married.

It was a Wednesday morning when I finally got around to calling Dan. I was stuck in West Hollywood rush-hour traffic and nobody on my "I'm bored and sitting in the car" phone sheet was available to talk, so I decided to try Dan. I didn't have any real questions. I guess I wanted to make sure that he wasn't scamming me, but more than that I just figured he must be really eager to get to know me.

After just two rings, a young voice with a distinctly Californian accent answered.

"This is Dan."

"Hey, Dan! It's Jenny!" I was so excited for him. He finally had me on the phone.

"Hi," he said, unmoved. "How can I help you?" It must have been hard for Dan to hold back his enthusiasm. How often was it that he got to talk to buyers directly? Especially ones that had googleable sex scenes on the Internet? It was kind of sweet that he was trying.

"I just wanted to talk through this whole thing with you before placing my order. The last guy I tried to do business with claimed I'd be eaten by lions if I didn't buy from him, so I'm just a little wary."

"Lions? Wow. Well, there are no lions here." Hmm. I was giving Dan room to banter with me and he was totally missing his cues. Dan wasn't as funny as I wanted him to be.

"Daaaaaaan. I'm from L.A. I just want my house to look like Irene Neuwirth's. Is this whole thing legit? Do you promise you aren't just trying to steal from me? The ladies on your site aren't just hanging out on a Universal Studios back lot, are they?"

"Ha." I smiled, pleased to finally get a rise out of him. "No, I assure you we are a real operation and we guarantee that the rug will arrive in one piece on your doorstep or your money back."

Then, a flash of inspiration. "You know, I'd love to come

there someday and see this operation. Is that possible?" I was only half-serious, half making sure he wasn't on a Universal Studios back lot.

He sounded skeptical. "You do realize the Berber people don't speak English."

"Do they speak French or German?"

"No."

"How about Spanish? I don't speak it, but I do know all the words to Madonna's 'La Isla Bonita.' Okay, don't tell anyone, but I also know one Pitbull song."

"They speak their own indigenous language. I'm sure you haven't heard it."

"That's cool. It might even be a plus. People usually love me when they can't understand a word I'm saying."

Dan paused, with what felt like disbelief.

"Yeah, I don't think you would enjoy yourself. Have you ever been camping?"

"No."

"Hiked a mountain?"

"Magic Mountain."

"Slept on the floor?"

"I was a theater major."

Dan chuckled, but it was obvious he'd never learned how to trust by closing his eyes and allowing his body to be lifted into the air by a group of fellow thespians. It was also obvious that he didn't want me to visit. Without coming straight out and saying it, Dan was implying that I couldn't hack it in the Atlas. He might have also been implying that I couldn't hack it as a theater major, but that could have just been my own projection.

Later that night, I bought the rug. Before bed, I lamented to Jason that the socially inept stranger I met online wasn't completely in love with me, and I told him how he laughed at the idea of me coming to the Atlas Mountains to see the weavers. I was looking for support, but Jason just rolled his eyes and sidled into bed beside me.

"Oh, I'm sure you could hack it, Anderson Cooper. Sounds like just the kind of trip I could see you taking."

The sarcasm stung, but I refrained from engaging.

The next morning, I did some research. Here's what I learned. The co-op was five hours outside Marrakech, deep in the Atlas Mountains. If I were to go, I'd have to fly to Africa, make my way through Casablanca, get on a smaller plane to Marrakech, hire a driver to take me five hours into the mountains, and hike three miles before even seeing a weaver. I'd never taken that kind of trip before. Usually my vacations consisted of sitting on a beach drinking overpriced iced tea and contemplating how I looked in a bikini. This would be a far more badass endeavor. The kind of story I could brag about one day to my son. Something I'd probably have to invest in waterproof boots for.

It was a few months later, in March, and we were staying in New York City. Jason was in previews for a Broadway show, and since I refused to sleep in the L.A. house alone, I was stuck on the East Coast with him. When I learned that my rug had at last been delivered back in L.A., I texted Lita to open up the colossal package in Sid's room in front of a smoke detector she hadn't realized was a nanny cam. Lita was a little alarmed to hear my voice come out of the detector, but she complied when I told her to move the rug a little to the left. From what I could see on the grainy screen, it was perfect.

"Fuck you, ABC Home!" I announced victoriously.

A few days later, I got a surprise message from Dan. He hadn't forgotten that I was interested in meeting his weavers—probably because I'd been texting him about it every two weeks. I'd been following their slowly burgeoning Instagram account, thinking about how many more likes they'd get if they understood lighting and the importance of high-angle shots with cute handbags. But more than daydreaming about how I could help these women, I selfishly thought about what they might offer me. The women in the photos seemed wise beyond their years, and not just because they didn't use sunscreen. Because they'd suffered hardships beyond anything my theater-school mind could even begin to improvise. They had nothing and yet everything. Their priorities were simple, uncluttered by the narcissism that creeps in once you own a magnifying mirror and an app that can erase wrinkles. They were profoundly pure and I yearned for their approval.

Dan had a proposition for me. If I was willing to post something on my social media accounts about The Anou and drum up some votes for a grant competition they were in, he would escort me to the co-op himself.

Delighted that Dan had finally googled me and deemed me an asset to the cause, I agreed. I posted a message on Twitter, my cyber friends stepped up to the challenge, and we promptly crashed the voting site. Unfortunately, because the majority of The Anou's votes came from outside Morocco, they were disqualified from the competition. But Dan assured me that a deal was a deal. If I was ready to visit, he'd be there to lead the way.

This was the opportunity I'd been waiting for, the chance to show Sid (and Jason, and Dan, and Mustapha) what I was capable of.

I knew right off the bat that I couldn't take Jason with me. He was working until August, and if I wanted to catch Dan, I had to be there by the end of April. And besides, I needed to do this without him. Jason had always booked my travel for me, even when we were dating. That was just the role in the relationship that he'd assumed. He was the planner and I was the doer. He was the hunter and I was the hunter's loud friend who gets drunk and accidentally shoots the hunter in the face with a crossbow. My biggest fear was that one day he'd die and I'd never know how to retrieve my American Airlines flight miles. Allowing Jason to help me with this trip would feel like cheating. And though I love cheating, I wanted this to be hard. I had something to prove, and I wasn't going to let Jason prove it for me.

I racked my brain trying to come up with a travel buddy who would offer no sense of security, and settled on my mom. The Moc was perfect for the trip. She loved new experiences, didn't mind getting dirty, and she'd emotionally abandoned me years ago.

"I'm sorry, Choppy, but I am way too blond and waaay too cute to go to Morocco." Her phone crackled as she spoke like I'd caught her mid-blowout.

"You're also sixty years old, Mom. Nobody wants you anymore," I said, listening to a round brush rip its way through her thin blond hair.

"Yes, they do. You should see the looks I get at the dog park." I loved it when she bragged to me about things that happened at the dog park, like it was an exclusive club I should be dying to get into.

"You have to come, because Jason won't let me go alone."

"I can't. They hate women and they hate our president."

My mom was oblivious when it came to global politics, but that never stopped her from having strong opinions. After ten years of marriage to John, a staunch Republican from the Midwest, she now sends texts saying things like, "When Bruce Jenner cuts off his balls, he should give them to Obama."

I told her I'd give her a few days to think about my offer and that we'd talk later in the week. Two hours later, she forwarded me a Fox News article about how ISIS was planning to launch an attack on the tourist economy in Tunisia.

"Sorry, Choppy, but I talked to John and we think it's too dangerous. I just attract way too much attention."

I considered calling her and explaining that Morocco and Tunisia were, in fact, separate countries that didn't even border each other, but I could already imagine the back-and-forth and it sounded worse than getting blown apart in Tunisia.

Then, a thought: Randolph and Brandon. They weren't friends I'd initially considered; we weren't extraordinarily close, and up until recently, we lived on opposite coasts. But the more I thought about it, the more I realized all my other options would be people I'd have to pay for.

Randolph was twenty-six years old and half-Filipino, with porcelain skin and hips I'm still waiting to get from Pilates. He was independently wealthy, and the only job he'd ever held was COO of his mother's walk-in closet. He grew up an only child in South Beach, Miami, and had been openly gay since high school. He'd moved to New York when he was eighteen in the hope of meeting the man of his dreams and possibly becoming the villain on a reality show.

I'd met Randolph five years earlier while on vacation on the Amalfi coast. Jason had just spent three months working on a movie and I'd just spent three days working on a tweet. We were both exhausted. I was lying by the pool, trying to compose the best picture of my feet on vacation, when out of nowhere, an evenly bronzed Asian boy in giant Yves Saint Laurent sunglasses and a Versace Speedo approached us.

"Hi, I know you're on vacation and I don't want to bother you, but I just wanted to say that I'm a huge fan."

"That's so cool. Thank you," Jason said, turning on the charm.

The fashionista paused. "Oh, not you. Your wife. Jenny? From Twitter?"

Jason's face dropped as I sprang out of my chair like I'd been crowned Miss America. This was the first time in my life I'd been recognized by a stranger (aside from the time I worked with Skeet Ulrich on *Law & Order: LA* and he recognized me as "that girl who brings her dog with her to the gym").

"What's your name?" I shrieked, trying to hold back tears of excitement.

"I'm Randolph, and that's my boyfriend, Brandon."

He pointed to a six-foot-two Jewish Clark Kent with a towel around his neck. There was something about Brandon that I could tell immediately disarmed Jason. If Randolph was the creepy guy sitting alone near the playground, Brandon was the wife and kids that just arrived, instantly transforming him into somebody you'd leave alone with your stroller. Maybe it was the fact that he was from the same county in New Jersey or that he didn't know what a "@jennyandteets" was. Either way, Jason was assuaged. The four of us had dinner that night and we'd stayed in touch ever since.

When I mentioned inviting Randolph and Brandon to join me in Morocco Jason was relieved. Like Jason, Brandon was a planner, and if things got out of hand, he knew how to call an American Express travel concierge for help.

Brandon and Randolph called me on speakerphone to hash out the logistics. They first asked about where we were staying. I couldn't offer many details because I didn't know the co-op's exact location. I didn't know the name of any neighboring towns, nor did I have coordinates on a map. According to Dan, I told Brandon, the weavers' location was deliberately concealed to protect them from opportunists looking to scam them out of their profits.

"Wait, who's Dan?" Brandon said, trying to process.

"He's a guy she met online. *It's fine,*" Randolph huffed, impatient. "We are in. What should I wear?"

"Well, it could be horribly cold or brutally hot, so I'm bringing a sweater, some jean shorts, Jason's ex's caftan, and a pair of gladiator sandals."

"Don't say the Isabel Marant ones with the rhinestones, because I'm dying for those! I gotta go shopping." Randolph started to pant, aroused.

Everything was falling into place. There was just one small roadblock standing in my way. I forgot that I'd invited my good friend/ex-boyfriend's ex-girlfriend Kate to come see *Hedwig and the Angry Inch* on Broadway with me in a week. It was her favorite musical and I knew a guy who could get us backstage. I didn't want to disappoint Kate. We'd had the same penis inside us and it was disappointing enough. Kate had been such an incredible friend to me over the years. We were practically sisters. Penis sisters. I wasn't going to let her down.

In order to accommodate Kate and still make my trip, I needed to be back in New York by April 11. Brandon and Randolph were going to be in London on business until the seventh, but were willing to meet me in Marrakech on the eighth. I couldn't find a flight that would get me in on the eighth, and I had too much pride to ask Jason for help (especially after asking him to get me backstage at *Hedwig*), so I booked myself on a flight for the sixth. That would mean one night alone in Marrakech. The idea was just unsettling enough to get me excited.

"You see," I later explained to Jason, "in order to understand the mountains, I first have to understand the city."

"Whatever you say, Anderson. You know the front lines better than anyone."

As time drew closer, I started to get nervous about my itinerary. Dan intermittently responded to my e-mails, but he was always vague. Maybe my mom was right. Maybe Morocco was dangerous. Maybe it was teeming with terrorists. I pictured myself with a pillowcase over my head in an abandoned bomb shelter, pleading with my would-be attackers.

"Hey, so I know you guys are extremists or whatever, but have you seen *Hedwig and the Angry Inch*? Because I have tickets for this Saturday, and if I'm not there my penis sister is gonna be furious. What? Oh, you know, a penis sister. Yeah, it's like when you are bonded for life because you've both had the same penis inside you. Not *at the same time. Allahu akbar,* calm down."

⟋

When the day finally came, I was no more prepared than I'd been two weeks prior. Sid was on the floor, screaming hysterically because his nanny, Naomi, wouldn't let him chase Teets around the apartment with a spork. I swept him into my arms and tried not to cry as I kissed him goodbye, promising I'd be back soon. Naomi assured me that he would be fine with her and Daddy. I knew she was right, but that didn't stop my body from wanting to shit and throw up at the exact same time.

By the time I'd reached the airport, my anxiety about Morocco had lessened to a mild apprehension that was easily ameliorated with a glass of champagne and an Ambien. I boarded the plane, settled into my seat, and drifted into a pleasant sleep.

When we landed in Marrakech, I vanished into the circuitous sea of immigration desks. Once my passport was stamped, I got in a car and headed to my hotel. Outside, beat-up cars zipped through the terra-cotta-colored streets. Groups of men sat on sprawling blankets selling souvenirs and peanuts. It felt sort of like Mexico but without the Chiclets. If you've been to Mexico, then you've basically been to Romania, Morocco, Turkey, Greece. Through the eyes of an American they sort of blend together. Worn-down buildings, outdated ad campaigns starring Monica Bellucci, everyone drinking Coca-Cola Lite. I appreciated its authenticity, but I couldn't help feeling superior.

Check-in was easy—so easy that I started to get cocky. Skipping down the long mahogany hall to my room, I praised myself for making the decision to come to Morocco. I missed Sid, but in that moment I missed my old life more. I was the old Jenny again—the young Jenny, the fun Jenny, the impulsive Jenny who did completely impractical, thoroughly ill-advised things because they'd make a good story. It felt right, like slipping into a pair of jeans you haven't been able to button since college.

I walked through an intimidating archway into a modestly sized suite steeped in rich reds and dark greens. An arabesque lattice screen divided the open tiled shower from an intricately carved bed. At the foot sat a silver tray holding a plate of fresh dates and a glass of lavender-scented almond milk. I was in heaven. Muslim heaven—the kind they promise suicide bombers. From my window I could see the top of the iconic Koutoubia Mosque jutting out from Medina Square.

I opened my roller bag and changed clothes for a victory lap around town. Tragically, I hadn't thought a lot about what I'd wear when I packed. I just sort of piled a bunch of colorful scarves and peasant tops in a bag and figured I'd piece together a look once I arrived. But no matter how I mixed and matched, I still wound up looking like a Wise Man from a Nativity scene. I settled on a long skirt, a tank top, and two equally offensive scarves.

Too self-conscious to stop at the front desk and ask for directions, I covered my face with one of the scarves, turning it into a makeshift hijab, and sheepishly walked out the front door.

I waited fifteen minutes for a break in traffic, then crossed the street to the Koutoubia Gardens. I hadn't been walking more than a few seconds when a man with dark eyes and a goatee noticed me. He looked like a mixture of my last Uber driver and a bad guy from the movie *Taken*.

"Hey, hello! Excuse me."

Ignoring him, I kept walking.

"It's me, Ussama! Remember? From the hotel? I just helped you check in," he said in a tone that implied I was a racist for not picking him out of the crowd.

"Oh, sorry. I didn't recognize you for a minute because I'm jet-lagged," I lied.

"I'm also in my street clothes now." He smiled, looking down at his tight-fitting jeans and inappropriately warm Patagonia puffy vest. "I'm heading into the main square to meet my wife and twin daughters."

Before he finished sounding out the word "daughters," I had my phone out and was showing him pictures of Sid.

"I have a son. He's one. This is him at the park and this is him trying to press his penis back inside his body. He loves buttons."

Ussama ignored me like a bad actor too attached to the script.

"So, you going shopping in the souks? You looking to buy a rug?"

"No, I actually already have one. I'm going to the mountains to meet the women that made it. Today I'm just looking around." I started to sense where the conversation was heading.

"Mountains is a dangerous place for a delicate flower like yourself."

Satisfied that I'd been mistaken for a delicate flower but annoyed that another man was telling me I couldn't handle myself, I started to lose patience.

"I think I can go it alone from here; thanks for your help." I started to move away, but he pressed on.

"You are lucky. Today is the last day of the Berber market. Real Berber rugs. Tomorrow? You won't be able to find them. You have good luck. Come, I'll show you." Ussama led me through the Koutoubia Gardens with a phony grin on his face. I studied his eyes, convinced now that he didn't work at my hotel or any other.

I'd learned on a trip to Istanbul that when someone tells you they are taking you to a special market, they are probably taking you to an alley to rape you. Not that I was ever actually raped. I had been with Jason and cornered by a menacing local when a group of shoeless children playing soccer with an empty soda can distracted our would-be assailant by spitting on his Members Only jacket, and we narrowly escaped. Maybe the guy was just planning on robbing us, or maybe he was planning on decapitating Jason and fucking me with his dismembered head. I'll never really know. The point is, I knew there was no Berber market.

As he grabbed my arm, towing me unwillingly past horse-drawn carriages and kids on motorbikes, I was furious with myself. I'd been outside the gates of my hotel for only a few minutes and already I'd allowed myself to be *Taken*. I'd just confirmed every fear about my own incompetence that I'd come to Morocco to disprove. That was it. There was no way in fuck I was gonna let Ussama scam me or rob me or *take* me.

Ussama dragged me across five lanes of traffic toward a large steel unmarked door.

"Go inside, have a look," he said eagerly.

"NO," I barked, the way my mom taught me to do if a stranger ever asked to touch my vagina.

Ussama was taken aback by my sudden shift toward bluntness. I, too, was rattled by my surge of self-possession. I wasn't normally the girl who asserted herself at the expense of someone else's feelings. I was the girl who would French-kiss a guy I never planned on seeing again just to extricate myself from a date faster. Proud of myself for taking a stand, I hustled off in the opposite direction.

When I was out of sight, my phone rang. It was Joan Arthur.

"HONNNNNNNNEEEEEEY! I just went to Joan's on Third for a fifteen-dollar juice and, honey? Joan got fat."

"Honey? I almost just got *Taken* in Morocco. But I'm in the clear now."

"What? Oh, shit, girl. Where are you? Do you know?"

"Not really." I looked around, trying to get my bearings. "I'm surrounded by lamps. Lots of brass lamps. And I think I just saw the hind legs of a donkey get pushed by in a wheelbarrow."

"Hold on, girl, I'm pulling you up on Google Earth." I waited. "Are you in the medina?"

"Yes," I said confidently. I was Carrie Mathison on the phone with Saul Berenson.

"Turn right," she demanded. "What do you see?"

"I'm in the middle of a market." I looked around and realized I was standing at the center of Jemaa el-Fnaa, the heart of the medina. The open arena was filled with oversize orange-juice stands, men selling teeth, monkey tamers, snake charmers, henna-tattoo artists, and child laborers. I was safe. Before I could tell Joan, a European woman asked if I'd mind posing for a picture with her daughter. I hung up on Joan and agreed, thrilled to be recognized so far from home.

"Thanks, Princess Jasmine," the little girl gushed.

Rattled by the encounter with Ussama and the fact that my ensemble got me mistaken for a Disney princess, I hurried back to my hotel, stifling tears. By the time I got there, my fear had turned to anger. I walked up to the concierge with conviction.

"Hi, I'm here for two more days and I'm gonna need a full-time guide. In fact, I should probably have eyes on me at all times."

"Yes, madame, I find you guide. You looking for rug? He get best price," the concierge said in a scheming tone.

"I already have one!" I fumed.

I tried to stay strong, but I couldn't help feeling defeated. I was a stranger in a strange land where even the good guys wanted to overcharge me for a rug.

"By the way, does a guy named Ussama work here?"

"No."

"Didn't think so," I said defiantly, sweeping my scarves off my face and storming off.

Instead of heading up to my room, I decided to stop by the garden to caffeinate and devise a new plan of attack. Three German teenage boys sat with their parents to my right, and I eavesdropped as they tried to translate the menu for their mother.

"Nein, chevre chaud bedeutet heiss! Heisse Käse."

Behind me sat a glamorous older Frenchwoman in white

linen pants and a navy blazer. She ate a plate of smoked salmon with crème fraîche and toast points as a small terrier peeked out beneath her feet. I ordered a coffee and stared at her terrier.

"*Bonjour,*" the woman said, and nodded.

"*Bonjour.* Your dog is so cute. I didn't know the hotel allowed pets." I didn't even try to speak to her in French. My outfit was humiliating enough.

"Oh, umm . . ." She paused to translate her thoughts into English. "Fifi is not mine. She is a VIP. She belongs to a friend of mine. I'm just watching her for a few hours."

Charlotte was from Paris, I learned. She was seventy-five and still sexy, with long, lean legs and a short gray shag. Her face wasn't pulled or peeled in any attempt to fight gravity. She wore her wrinkles proudly. I had a fantasy of one day doing the same, immediately followed by a fantasy of doing the exact opposite. Charlotte was discreet about the nature of her trip but did mention she had friends in the city and traveled there often. I told her about my experience with Ussama in the medina and she was empathetic but also unsurprised.

"The thing you must remember about Moroccans is that everyone is lying to you at all times." She shook her head in disappointment. Charlotte implored me to give the city another chance and offered to take me on a tour after I finished my lunch. I eagerly accepted.

When I'd paid my check, I found Charlotte outside with Fifi and two older Frenchmen. Jean Georges was elegant and tan in a crisp white button-down and black trousers. His lover, Florent, was more portly and flamboyant, donning coral-colored culottes and pointy Moroccan slippers. The men didn't speak English, forcing me to butcher a language I'd spent seven school years trying to master. As the afternoon sun began to set over a clear desert sky, we walked leisurely through the park I'd felt intimidated in hours earlier. The weather was warm, ideal for someone dressed like Lawrence of Arabia. Water sellers in bright red costumes with large Berber hats stood by the entrance, clanking copper cups and asking for spare change.

Charlotte was explaining to me that her friends lived in Paris but spent a good portion of their time at a small *riad* they owned in the souks, near the markets of Marrakech. For Parisians, Marrakech was just a three-hour plane ride and an ideal place to own property. It was sunny and spacious, and offered all the luxury you'd find in the South of France for half the price. At first it seemed a strange choice, two openly gay men wanting a vacation home in a predominantly Muslim country. But as I looked around, I saw gay men everywhere. On a scale of one to gay, I would say Marrakech ranked just above Palm Springs and just below Mykonos. It was only my second time outside the hotel and already the city took on a different persona. Young lovers laughed and frolicked in the streets. Children hung off their mothers' legs, begging for crescent-shaped cookies filled with almond paste. It was as if my first impression was a test. Now that I'd passed, the city shed its ominous veneer and was willing to show me its splendor.

We arrived at Jean Georges and Florent's *riad* deep in the souks. A labyrinth of passageways on either side led to vendors selling plastic jugs of argan oil, piles of vividly colored spices, cheap metals, lamb innards, dried fruits, silk fabrics, and everything you've seen in the jewelry section at Cost Plus World Market. We made our way up to the roof of their narrow four-story compound and looked out on the sprawling maze below.

Charlotte pointed to different buildings and told me their origins. She explained to me why Morocco was such a safe place.

"Everyone here is a spy. They are all informants for the king. Nothing bad is allowed to happen to tourists. They want the tourists to stay and spend money. You understand?"

I didn't even know Morocco *had* a king, but I nodded as if I understood completely. Fifi could tell I was lying.

Jean Georges offered me an espresso, which I gladly accepted. Florent held out a bowl of bonbons.

"Oh, no, *merci*. I'm from L.A.," I said, certain he'd understand.

Charlotte's phone rang and she answered it. After exchanging a few quick words, she hung up and told me that a chauffeur was on his way to the *riad* to pick up the terrier.

"If you prefer, you can ride *avec* Fifi back to the hotel," she offered.

Fifi looked at me, then back at Charlotte. She either didn't like the plan or was offended she hadn't yet been offered a bonbon. Florent let out a laugh.

"Royal doggy," he said, and snickered.

Charlotte shrugged. "You see, Fifi belongs to the king's grandmother. That is my friend. We are all friends of the royal palace. You understand?"

"Completely." I nodded knowingly. I didn't understand at all.

When Fifi's chauffeur arrived, she jumped in the front seat and I was relegated to the back. I could see Charlotte and the boys on the rooftop, waving.

"You are fine! Nobody is going to rape you!" she called out. "The king knows you're here!" Her words reverberated off the narrow alley walls as the car reversed down the cobbled street and into the sunset.

〜

That night, I googled the king of Morocco. He seemed chill. And I felt safer having met Charlotte. I was grateful for her hospitality. When you're traveling with another person, you're inevitably cut off from certain experiences. People don't invite you to coffee at their *riads* or notify the king of your presence. They assume you and your companion want to be left alone, even though you're screaming at him because he can't take a single picture of you without making you look like your dad in a wig. On your own, the possibilities are limitless and only the most flattering pics get uploaded to your iCloud.

Before bed, I sent Dan another e-mail confirming that we were still seeing each other in the morning. He responded and told me he'd meet me in my lobby at eleven. I gave him the address and notified him that Randolph and Brandon would be getting in around the same time. Once we were all together, the plan was to get in a car immediately and drive out to the Atlas Mountains. I hoped Dan understood that "immediately" meant "immediately after stopping for coffee and snacks." His demeanor made it hard to tell if he was someone who, like me, needs to eat every couple hours, or if he was a robot.

I woke up early the next morning, buzzing with excitement. Knowing Randolph would crucify me if I walked into the lobby looking like Jesus of Nazareth, I toned down the scarves and tried for a subtler look. I still had my army-green pants that I'd worn on the plane. They were dirty, but I figured where we were heading was dirtier. I paired the pants with a suede leather jacket I brought in case it got cold and a large brimmed hat. Now instead of looking like I'd dreamed of Jeannie I looked like Crocodile Dundee. Downstairs, I wandered around the foyer, admiring the tapestries and waiting for Dan and my gays.

"Jenny?"

I turned to find a lanky white guy and a young Moroccan girl walking toward me.

"Daaaaaan!"

He was exactly how I'd pictured him: athletic, aloof, low-maintenance. He seemed like the type of guy who eats that sugar-gel shit they sell at the checkout counter in outdoor adventure stores. I'd bet my house he owned a pair of web-footed running shoes and a Dave Matthews *Live at Red Rocks* CD.

"Hey, happy you made it," he said in a tone that suggested he still had zero interest in falling madly in love with me.

Before I had a chance to meet his companion, Brandon and Randolph appeared. Brandon looked disoriented and dizzy, like a runner-up on *The Amazing Race,* but Randolph was unruffled in his seersucker shorts, silk shirt, and Hermès ascot.

"Ugh, I have the worst service in here." Randolph tore off his cat's-eye sunglasses and whisked his bangs from his face. "We were trying to call." He banged on his phone, then looked up at me quizzically.

"Why are you dressed like John Wayne?"

"Am I?" I feigned ignorance and changed the subject. "Hi, I'm Jenny," I said, extending my hand to the young Moroccan who'd accompanied Dan.

"I'm Dan's partner, Tifa. I think we spoke on the phone."

She blushed, making it impossible to tell if "partner" meant business or romantic. If Dan and Tifa were having sex, I pictured it to be the way fish do, where they just circle each other, chest-bumping.

With introductions out of the way, our group was assembled and ready to go. We took our bags outside and waited for our car to arrive.

I pointed out the park to Randolph. Sitting on a bench was Ussama. He saw me and I waved.

"That's Ussama. He tried to *Take* me on my first day, but now I think we're cool. Apparently, Marrakech is totally safe. Also, I think the king knows I'm here. It's a whole thing."

Randolph tried to focus, but he couldn't get past my outfit.

"I just don't understand—" he said, shielding his eyes from the sun with an arm wrapped in Cartier love bracelets.

"Me neither. It might just be a figure of speech."

Capitalizing on the few extra minutes, Brandon sneaked back inside to the restroom to wash his face and apply a cucumber eye gel. Dan and Tifa stood in the road and waved down a Mercedes adorned in vintage stickers that looked like it just rolled off the set of a Wes Anderson film.

The car stopped in front of us and I waited for Bill Murray to pop out. Instead, a man named Doud appeared. He was built like a bouncer, with a black turban and a large bristly mustache that covered the majority of his face. He didn't speak English, just grunted and scowled.

"Everybody ready?" Dan said cheerily.

I could already tell Dan was on a different planet when it came to simple comforts. He and Tifa hopped in the front seat with Doud, while Brandon, Randolph, and I squeezed into the back. When all the doors were shut and the car started moving, I turned into the person I turn into on airplanes: a ravenous trapped animal.

"Did anyone bring snacks? I just got hungry."

Brandon, the only other Jew in the car, shared my concern. He revealed a small packet of Marcona almonds.

"I brought these from London, if you want some."

"YES." I reached over Randolph and took a handful.

"We're gonna stop at, like, a deli or something, right?" Brandon inquired nervously.

There's nothing more disconcerting than not knowing when you're going to eat again.

Like sometimes even just going to bed at night stresses me out. I stared out the window, on the lookout for a modest but authentic kebab place.

Dan looked back at us, then said something I couldn't hear over the blaring Berber folk music blasting from Doud's crushed velvet speakers.

"Apparently, dinner is going to be waiting for us when we arrive," Brandon relayed giddily.

We drove for five hours straight. At one point I asked if we could stop the car to pee, but Dan wasn't receptive. Doud mumbled a few words in Tamazight, his native tongue, then shook his head no. Dan explained that stopping to pee in rural Morocco was never a good idea. You might feel like you're alone. You might not have seen a single soul for miles. But the minute you walk behind a bush to relieve yourself, there is almost always somebody standing behind you, watching.

"That's what makes these mountains so safe. They are actually swarming with people. You just can't see them." The way

Dan described it, it sounded like there were families of Berbers living under every rock. I couldn't decide if these new insights made me feel safer, but out of respect, I held my bladder.

At last, Doud stopped the car on the side of a cliff near a sign that said GITE AZOUL. I looked around, confused. There was nothing but a vast red canyon with a single minaret far in the distance and a creepy expressionless man holding a sickle standing behind a bush watching us. I tried not to make eye contact as I looked out at the green valley flanked on all sides by picturesque alpine peaks. The air was crisp and clean and confusing to my Angeleno lungs.

"We're here," Tifa said.

"We are?" I could tell Brandon was already on hold with American Express in his mind.

"It's just a small hike down," Dan said, smiling and waving at the creepy man with the sickle.

"Do you know him?" I inquired.

"Yeah, good guy. He's hilarious."

Doud pulled our suitcases out of the Mercedes's cavernous trunk and smiled at us with a mouth full of silver before getting back into his car and taking off.

"Wait," I cried. "Are you sure we don't need him anymore?"

It was too late. Doud was gone in one direction and Dan in the other.

Sliding down the rocky cliff in UGG boots that were meant for sitting in the Coffee Bean on Sunset, it started to dawn on me that when Dan said something was a small journey away, he actually meant that if you had any preexisting health conditions you probably shouldn't follow.

Dan was pumped when, after what felt like four miles of

rock jumping but might have been four minutes, we arrived at our destination. A man he called Danger walked out to greet us. He nodded hello as a clambering rooster writhed in his arms. The three-story concrete home was an impressive departure from the surrounding structures and, according to a later Zillow search, the most expensive home on the mountain.

"What's for dinner?" Brandon asked, salivating like a Labrador at an outdoor café.

"Probably one of those." Dan pointed toward a small pen containing an emaciated cow and a small goat.

"So it isn't ready yet?" I panicked.

Inside the concrete compound, a woman and her two sons stood in an open kitchen, brewing tea. It was dark save for a single lightbulb that swung from the ceiling. Danger escorted us down a long, dilapidated corridor that smelled like a soaking wet suit forgotten in the trunk of a car. Looking up, I could see twigs and branches peeking through the newly plastered roof, vestiges of a more provincial time. Danger beamed with pride as Dan explained to us that when he first started visiting the valley years ago, Danger lived in a hut like everybody else, but after four years of opening his home to travelers, he had saved enough money to build the palace we were standing in.

We were escorted into a room where I imagine Osama bin Laden had at some point been hidden. In a corner of the empty, carpeted space was a pile of rugs and two large pieces of foam.

"Oh, yeah! I get so excited when I get a bed." Dan looked at Tifa, extending his hand for a high five. She obliged, but I could tell that part of her hated Dan.

I didn't know whether to laugh or cry. I knew I was looking

for a test of my bravery that I could share with my son, but I wasn't expecting to do an overnight at what looked like the honeymoon suite at a Taliban training camp. Brandon's face lost all color as he peeked around the corner at the bathroom.

"Guys? There's no toilet."

Dan and Danger exchanged a few words.

"Yeah, they still use squat toilets. Oh, and I guess the water isn't working right now, but hopefully in the morning." I realized that Dan guaranteeing something was pretty much a sure way to know it was never going to happen.

"I once used a toilet like that in China and ended up shitting on my feet," I confided to Randolph.

"Brandon doesn't know I shit," Randolph replied matter-of-factly.

After being shown our rooms, Tifa, Randolph, and I settled into the main salon just off the kitchen. Large picture windows showcased the lushness of a land untouched by time. Randolph waited until Dan was out of earshot before interrogating Tifa.

"So are you guys like a couple? Or did you ever have a crush on each other or—"

"I have a crush on everybody I meet," Tifa cut in. "I even have a small crush on you." She looked at him and giggled.

"Aw, I love this girl!" Randolph gently patted Tifa on the back as though she were a puppy he found in a box on the side of the road and that probably had rabies.

Dan entered the room with Danger trailing behind him.

"Dinner is ready! And I think we got the cow!" He took his laptop off the table and a small *tagine* was placed in its center.

"There isn't any silverware, so we all have to use our hands."

Tifa grabbed a triangle of bread out of a straw basket and scooped up a bit of olive and onions. Under the blanket of vegetables hid a small pile of bones. I think they might have belonged to a chinchilla. I laid claim to the largest section of flesh I could find and quickly stuffed it in my mouth to establish that I was the pack leader. "Are we *sure* this is the cow?"

Randolph peered out the window, but it was too dark to see if the cow was missing.

"I could live on olives," Dan said, popping a single olive in his mouth, then kicking back in his chair as if he was now full.

Randolph and I scarfed down what was left of the tagine as the rest of the group watched.

"You two are way more adventurous than I am," Brandon said. "What if you get sick?" He stuck a stick of butter between two pieces of bread and made a sandwich.

"I want to get sick!" I said. "I still have baby fat to lose."

"Me, too!" Randolph pinched his perfectly round cheeks, causing a bit of marrow to peek out of the corner of his mouth.

After dinner, Dan walked us through the schedule for the morning. A car would pick us up at seven and take us to the co-op. Around 3 p.m., a different car would retrieve us and drive us back to Danger's house to get our things, where yet another car would be waiting to return us safely to Marrakech. The plan seemed reasonable. Though he'd grossly oversold the lodging situation, I still trusted that Dan had everything under control.

When it got too dark in the room to make direct eye contact, the group started to disperse. Dan reached his arms up and fake-yawned, then bid us good night. Tifa followed, but not before making it very clear that they were sleeping in separate rooms. Brandon popped a melatonin, slipped into a matching silk pajama set, and disappeared into the Osama chamber.

I was tired, but Randolph was wide awake and wanted to talk about the people we both hated on Twitter. I was more interested in our host.

"Wait," I said, "can we revisit the Dan subject again? Why isn't he more into us? And, I mean, he isn't just some asshole posting selfies with a piece of paper that says #JeSuisCharlie. He's like a real-life humanitarian who doesn't even have a Facebook page. There's obviously something deeply wrong with him. What do you think it is?"

"Do you think that he hates us?" Randolph said under his breath.

"I wish! I don't think he even cares about us enough to hate us."

It was pitch black, and I'd followed an indifferent stranger into the middle of nowhere. I scolded myself for not having prepared myself better for this trip. For not being more like Jason and doing my research. And why was I there? So I could prove that I was capable? Capable of getting lost?

My eyes were bloodshot and my clothes unchanged when we met Dan and Tifa in the dining area for breakfast. The rooster we'd seen in Danger's arms the night before wasn't making a sound, which explained our dinner. Randolph and I had stayed up all night, eating argan-oil crackers and discussing how even Miranda must think she is the Carrie of her group.

We waited an hour, bleary-eyed, for the van taking us to Ait Bouguemez, but it never arrived. Dan stepped out, then returned.

"So, I spoke with Danger and he said we missed the van. Guess it came earlier today," he said casually.

"Earlier? When? Is there another car we can get? Where's Doud?" I was going to be pissed if I'd come all this way just to eat a fucking rooster. Dan was killing me.

"Doud had to go pick up some people in the Sahara."

"Doud drove directly from us to the Sahara? How does that even make sense?" If only I'd stayed in Doud's Mercedes, I'd be relaxing in a casbah in Ouarzazate, smoking a strawberry-flavored hookah.

He ignored my question. "That van is the only car coming through for the day. If you guys are up for it we can walk to the next town over and see if we can catch a lift there. It's only six miles."

Two and a half hours later, we were still walking. Patches of neatly cut grass that looked like putting greens stretched alongside roaring white rapids. Tifa explained that flocks of grazing sheep were responsible for the grass's manicured appearance.

I started to feel like we were walking in a loop. There was little protection from the sun as the temperature started to build. Randolph was sweating through his ascot. I made eye contact with a woman and her child who stood stoically on the edge of the road, collecting firewood. Instantly I felt a pang of grief. I missed my own child. I wondered if he noticed I was gone or if he was anticipating my return or if he was already trying to *Parent Trap* Jason into meeting a new, more suitable mom, someone with less ambition and more self-esteem, or else just a killer blueberry muffin recipe.

Brandon's cell service started working and he immediately called his travel agent.

"Yes, two rooms and three massages. Tonight. We get in around seven. Jenny? You like your hotel in Marrakech? Because we're going back, baby!" He clicked his heels in the air clumsily, like a leprechaun desperate to take a shit. None of us had been able to release our bowels at Danger's house. I'd squatted over the hole twice and even played a Sia song on my iPhone to relax me, but nothing came out.

We were backed up with bread and baking in the sun when a large windowless van drove past.

"Stop! Wait!" I threw myself into the road. The van pulled over and Dan asked the driver if we could hitch a ride. A local nodded for us to get in.

"Are we sure this is safe?" Randolph looked into the dark space covered on all sides with aluminum paneling. The double doors shut behind us, and I couldn't help but wonder if they'd ever open again. The van threw us from side to side as it traveled up the washboard road to Ait Bouguemez. We were so close.

At last, the large metal doors opened and we all filed out. Across seventy acres of row crops sat a small concrete building on the top of the mountain. The words TAPIS BERBÈRES were spray-painted in white on the outside. It was the building I'd seen in all the pictures online, sometimes steeped in snow, other times brittle and parched in the high desert sun. This was the birthplace of my Beni Ourain. I wished Sid could see me. I accomplished what I'd set out to do. I pushed further than I thought I could go. I had held my bladder for an entire car ride, forgone a shower for twenty-four hours, slept on the floor, ingested rooster, and hitchhiked in a rape van to make it to this moment.

With newly restored conviction, I marched toward my weavers like a soldier returning from battle. My hands dug into the rocks as I climbed the last few feet to the co-op. My stomach was covered in dirt and my UGGs were dusty shells of their former selves, but I'd arrived.

"I'm heeeeere," I announced proudly, like I was the Fonz from *Happy Days*. A studio audience erupted into applause in my head as I brushed myself off and surveyed the scene.

I turned to my right, hoping to be greeted by cheerful throngs of leather-skinned mountain women, when an empty Coke can came flying at my head. Touching my cheek to make sure my filler hadn't shifted, I looked up at the culprit. Three giggling children stood above me on a rock, laughing. Their faces were rosy and their bellies were swollen (from carbs, not starvation). I picked up the can, which instructed me to share its contents with a "BFF," and walked farther into the co-op to go find one.

"Hello!" I called into the next room. "It's me, everyone! Jennyandteets!"

Inside, I found that the co-op was in fact a simple room of four concrete walls, buried in stacks and stacks of rugs. A long provincial loom with tiny strands of thread stood in its center. Ten Berber women sitting on the floor glanced over at me. None of them struck me as BFF material, but I tried to keep an open mind. An elderly woman with half-scribbled facial tattoos approached me and smiled. I tried to focus on her eyes instead of the erratic markings, which looked like she'd given Sid a pen and then left him alone in a room with her face.

Before I had a chance to connect my new BFF's face dots, Dan and Tifa appeared behind me to translate. Dan told the women that I was the lady from Los Angeles who'd ordered the large Beni Ourain.

"I am so happy to meet you guys! I've been looking at pictures of you for months." I used my hands to express myself. The woman and her fellow weavers shook their heads "no," trying to remind me that they didn't speak English. Tifa translated my enthusiasm, but they continued to stare at me blankly.

"So . . ." It had been only a couple minutes and I'd already run out of things to say. I craned my neck out the door, looking for Randolph and Brandon. The weavers continued with their work as if I weren't there. It wasn't every day that they got to meet one of their customers. Why weren't they interested? Weren't they impressed?

"Do you guys have any questions for me?" I ventured, trying to reclaim their attention.

Tifa and a younger woman combing cotton into a bucket exchanged several words, then Tifa looked at me and spoke.

"They want to know why you are here."

Caught off guard, I stopped for a beat and thought about it.

"Well, I . . ." It all made so much sense a minute ago, but now it was hard to articulate. "Originally it was because all these people kept telling me I couldn't. But I guess the root of why I'm here is to prove to myself that I have what it takes to be a good mother." It felt true, and yet it sounded so feeble as

I said it. Maybe I had secretly hoped that these rural women, who looked so rugged and fearsome in pictures, would tell me how impressed they were with me. How brave and courageous I was. How I was the most epic mom of all time.

I waited as Tifa translated. The women nodded, processing what she was saying. One of them fired back a question. I waited nervously for the translation.

"They want to know where your child is," Tifa said.

"Oh. He's in New York. I considered bringing him, but to be honest, this isn't really his scene." I glanced around the room. "No iPads."

Tifa stopped translating. She paused, then diplomatically explained that a Berber woman would never separate from her child. I turned to my side. An infant no more than a month old with a face that looked like a dehydrated apple lay swaddled and wedged between two carpets. Another weaver who I originally thought had a beer gut was actually wearing her sleeping toddler under her smock. I was surrounded by children. None of whom needed anything I had to offer. The one person who needed me was thousands of miles away, probably helping Jason eat blueberry muffin batter off his new girlfriend.

Realizing that the approval I so desperately craved was nowhere near this sub-alpine habitat, I stepped outside for the kind of boost to your mood that only a super-fashionable gay man can offer. Randolph was already waiting for me.

"We wanna go home. Nothing here is cute." He pouted like someone who had just waited in line for two hours for a sample sale that had nothing in his size.

"They'll custom-make you whatever you want—" I started to explain, before Dan interrupted.

"Guys, I'm afraid I have some bad news."

"Just tell them I'm Angelina Jolie and that this is my son Maddox," I said defensively, grabbing Randolph by the arm.

"The car that was supposed to pick us up is still in Marrakech and won't be here for at least five more hours."

Five hours. I was so over Dan. If my Coke can weren't empty, I would have poured it over his head.

Tifa suggested we leave the co-op and wait for our car elsewhere, as one of the weavers felt I was giving her the evil eye.

"Which one?" I looked around, paranoid.

"It doesn't matter," Tifa said reassuringly as we walked, reminding me that it is just a superstitious culture. Self-conscious and constipated, we wandered back down the mountain. We had barely crested the ridge on the far side of the valley when I spied a car. I squinted, trying to get a better look.

"Wait, is that—" The stickers on the trunk were a dead giveaway.

"You guys! That's Doud! DOUD!" I screamed, waving my hands for him to see us.

Dan tried to call Doud on his cell, but the number wasn't working. (I assumed Doud gave Dan a bogus number to avoid moments like these.) I felt like we were in the movie *Alive* and Doud was the last search party sent to find us. If he didn't pick us up, we'd be forgotten—condemned to wander the Atlas without food or Wi-Fi for at least another four and a half hours. We screamed and screamed, but his car only plowed ahead. Then, at last, Doud reached his hand out of the car and waved. He'd seen us.

"We're saved!" Randolph ran toward the car, flagging it down with his ascot. Victory music played in my head. We weren't going to have to find shelter, use any more data roaming, or eat Dan for survival.

Once we were back and safely tucked into our five-star resort, it was easier to appreciate all that we'd experienced (especially after we'd pooped out half of it). I felt closer to Randolph and Brandon for coming on the adventure with me, and though I was disappointed the Berber women didn't enlighten me as I'd hoped, meeting them did open my eyes to certain truths about myself. I realized I didn't actually enjoy feeling discomfort or having to plan vacations without the help of my husband-concierge. I realized that being an adult means not seeing every "no" as a challenge. And that traveling to the other side of the world wasn't going to help me escape the inadequacies I felt at home. Maybe Jason didn't doubt that I could make it to the mountains; he just knew I'd be annoyed when I discovered there was no iced tea or beach chair to take cute feet pics in. Maybe I wasn't meant to be Anderson Cooper flying to war zones, dodging bullets. Maybe Anderson Cooper wasn't what my son needed. I didn't want to raise a child who had to worry about his impulsive mother roaming the planet in search of PTSD. I wanted to raise a child who felt safe and secure enough to one day perform simulated sex on HBO.

Maybe I'm more like Brian Williams, turning everyday bravery into a war zone.

I waited patiently as my taxi driver honked his horn and screamed obscenities at a large van stopping traffic. My Air Maroc flight from Marrakech to Casablanca didn't board for another two hours, but I wanted to get to the airport early just to be safe. Brandon and Randolph decided to stay in Marrakech another two nights to check out the spa scene, but I had to get home to Sid and my penis sister.

Looking up from my phone, I noticed six Moroccan men huddled together on motorbikes, pointing at me and nodding. One held a Koran in his hand, the other a bottle of Jack Daniel's.

Unsettled, I locked my door and tried to think positive thoughts.

Teets riding a bicycle.

Teets riding a polar bear.

Teets riding a baby polar bear.

The cab had started moving slowly again, when suddenly the six men surrounded us. I screamed at the driver to take off, but there was nowhere to go. A hand had reached through the driver's window and unlocked the passenger-side door. Thinking fast, I did as Liam Neeson instructed and started screaming descriptions of each man at the top of my lungs.

"BEARD. FIVE FOOT TEN. PIERCED EAR. WHITE JEANS. TATTOO ON LEFT SHOULDER."

A pillowcase was thrown over my head before I could finish, as the men fastened me to the back of a bike. I started babbling to my abductor.

"Are you sex traffickers? You're probably looking for my mom; she's in San Diego. Are you guys ISIS? Am I being taken to an abandoned bomb shelter to make a video? Because you should know that anytime I'm uncomfortable I immediately start laughing uncontrollably. Like even when I see other people in pain."

The men shouted back and forth to one another as we buzzed through a network of crooked streets. From what seemed like above I heard sirens. Then, without warning, gunshots. The bike I was tied to spun out of control as a rocket-propelled grenade struck the vehicle in front of us. For a moment everything was dark. Then I came to, tearing the pillowcase off my head. My attacker was unconscious and bleeding next to his bike. I pulled myself out from under him and took off running down a dark alley. Before I could reach the end, a black SUV cut me off, stopping me in my tracks.

Doors opened on all sides and men in official uniforms seized me. I was too weak to ask questions. We drove in silence toward the desert, finally arriving at a large Moorish palace. The men in uniforms lifted me out of the car and escorted me through an archway into an opulent sitting room filled with vibrant silk pillows and rugs. I took a few deep breaths, shutting out the trauma of the last hour. I heard the creak of a door and turned to see the silhouette of a man veiled in shadows.

"Hello, Jenny. Would you care for some lavender-scented almond milk?"

A second man entered the room and set down a small tray before disappearing again into darkness.

"Who are you? Where am I?" I said.

The man stepped closer, his face now illuminated by sunlight.

"I'm the king of Morocco, Jenny. You still looking for a rug?"

6

MANHATTAN MARLBORO MYSTERY

It was May and Jason's play was nearing the end of its run. In less than four weeks we were supposed to be heading back to Los Angeles to set up shop for good. My nanny, Naomi, was eager to reunite with her family. Jason was anxious to play with his outdoor pizza oven. Sid was still too young to know where he was or how he got there. However, what all three of these important players had yet to realize was that I had no intention of ever going home.

I couldn't! Going home meant living in my haunted house. And though I'd promised Jason I'd try to find peace with the property, I'd realized after my trip to the Atlas Mountains that my home was the scariest place on the planet. I'd confronted my fears like they were playground bullies and lost not only my pride but also a year's worth of lunch money (on Etsy). As hard as I tried, I couldn't sweep my feelings under the rug, Moroccan or not.

I broke the news to Jason at sunset. The salty air clung to my skin as we wandered aimlessly down the Hudson River Greenway, waiting for our dogs to pee.

"I love it here," I started.

"Right? New York is the best!" Jason had been trying to sell me on New York from the day I met him. Raised just across the river in New Jersey, he was fiercely loyal to the city that blessed him with acting success at an early age and had gotten him away from his mother. To Jason, New York represented freedom, opportunity, and independence. We had all of those things in Los Angeles, but there was something about New York that brought Jason to life. I enjoyed the city, too, and romanticized it the way anyone who's ever seen a Woody Allen movie does. I never pictured myself growing old there (old people in New York look like they're made out of beef jerky), but I did enjoy picturing myself dressed like Annie Hall, walking the West Village, debating the absurdity and necessity of love.

"I think we should move here."

Jason looked at me, trying to figure out if I was serious. "You wouldn't."

"I've changed my mind. You've really sold me on the place," I said, knowing the first rule of persuading your husband to do something is making that thing seem like it's his idea.

"And you would be okay with seasons and not having the same amount of space? No yard, no pool, no pizza oven?"

"Well, lately I've started to question if houses and bread are really my thing. I think maybe I was just born to live the gluten-free condo life. One entrance, one exit, limited closet space, no scary driveways . . ."

"If this is just about the L.A. house—"

I stopped Jason before he could finish. It obviously *was* about the L.A. house, but I couldn't let him know that.

"NO! I'm sick of L.A. and I'm sick of your pizza—" I caught myself, but it was too late. "I mean . . . I love your pizza! You should totally open a restaurant chain. American Pies! We could make millions!"

Jason looked at me, incredulous.

"It's L.A. There's no depth there. I don't want Sid to turn into one of those privileged private-school assholes who wear James Perse, drink pressed juice, and buy their girlfriends micro-pavé jewelry from XIV Karats. I want him to walk places and wear Carter's and interact with Caribbean people."

Jason dropped the pizza debate and agreed that L.A. kids sucked. He also agreed that living in New York would undoubtedly offer more global exposure.

"You know I love it here. You don't have to sell me. But if we're really going to do this, I want you to be sure."

"I am," I said, praying I wasn't lying.

The truth was, I didn't know if Manhattan was the right answer. I just knew it was the answer for right now. I figured after my haunted house sold, I could always have a change of heart about the East Coast, hate the winter, become claustrophobic, miss my cryotherapist. But until then, I was determined to fall in love with the Big Apple.

Jason was overjoyed. The only person left to convince was my nanny, Naomi. Naomi was fifty-eight, with no children of her own. She had nieces in Los Angeles, but she also had an older sister in Brooklyn. I was never clear whom she liked better, but it felt good to know she had some kind of support system on both coasts. The bigger issue with New York was that it meant Naomi would be living in. Naomi never liked being a live-in nanny. She liked having her own apartment, her own car, and her own Bed Bath & Beyond coupons. I knew Naomi was fond of me, but I also knew how much her independence meant to her and how hard she'd worked to get it. This was a woman who got into the United States by riding across the Rio Grande on someone's back with only two dollars and a switchblade.

Before being granted political asylum in the United States, Naomi was a nurse and human rights activist in the mountains of Guatemala. She'd borne witness as her country's corrupt government took the lives of her brothers, lovers, and friends. After being torn off the street, kidnapped, and held at gunpoint, the militia threatened to kill the remaining members of her family if she didn't stop working for the opposition. She refused, and her family threw her on a bus bound for Mexico, hoping to save both her life and theirs. Naomi was a survivor. She was a fighter. New York didn't scare her. Ghosts didn't scare her. Not even sleeping six feet away from me scared her. (And I can get handsy.)

Jason and I proposed the plan to Naomi, and to our surprise, she was receptive. She'd grown to enjoy living together as a family and agreed that New York did present more opportunities for Sid.

Once the decision was made and the L.A. house was listed, a giant weight was lifted off my soul. I felt free again, or at least as free as I could feel with a baby. I'd narrowly escaped my ghost house, but I'd also narrowly escaped real adulthood. In New York I got to keep that piece of myself that Los Angeles tried to take away. Due to simple geography, L.A. forces you to choose between domesticity and freedom. After feeding and washing and rocking a child to sleep, the last thing you want to do is get in your car and drive for thirty minutes to eat a plate of jicama-wrapped guacamole. In Manhattan, I could be a mommy inside my apartment and, when the mood hit me, escape downstairs to a night out on the town complete with interactive theater and compost cookies from Momofuku Milk Bar. New York was like a giant cruise ship, one of the last remaining places where thirty-five was still considered young.

Naomi took two weeks off to pack up her life in L.A. and returned feeling liberated from the burden of car payments and electric bills. We were happy and hopeful and looking forward to the future when out of nowhere a cloud of doubt appeared—in my bedroom.

"I'm literally getting cancer as we speak!" I kvetched, as I crawled on my hands and knees along the floorboards, trying to sniff out where the scent had originated. There was no sign of anything on the floor. But I knew what I smelled: cigarette smoke. Naomi boosted me up with her hands so I could stick my head inside the air vent and detect if it was coming from upstairs. Still nothing. Whenever I called the building maintenance guy to investigate, the smoke would invariably stop. Then, usually right after dinner, it would kick in again. Jason tried to downplay the seriousness of the issue by pretending he couldn't smell anything.

"Jason! That's cigarette smoke! How do you not smell it?" I said, stomping neurotically around the room.

Jason stopping flossing his teeth to film me, the same way I filmed Sid whenever he threw an unwarranted tantrum in public.

"Baby, this is an old building. The smell is just part of the charm. It's probably just in the wood. And I don't even smell it, anyway."

"Naomi! There was cigarette smoke trapped in here earlier. You smelled it, right?" Naomi had been a live-in for less than a week and already I was triangulating her in every fight.

Naomi nodded her head yes, then ducked out of view in order to avoid landing on Jason's Instagram page.

"Have I mentioned yet that you need to get back on Zoloft?"

"I'm telling you, Jason, someone is smoking in this building and I'm going to find out who," I vowed, straight to camera.

After kissing Naomi good night, I took a shower and got into bed next to Jason, who I didn't plan on kissing for at least the next five years. I racked my brain, trying to piece together the mystery, but none of the facts added up. To my knowledge nobody in our building smoked. And the fact that the smell ebbed and flowed implied that it wasn't just a permanent feature of the apartment. Somebody somewhere was lighting up! The later it got, the crazier I felt. Maybe Jason was right. Maybe the smoke wasn't coming from an outside source. Maybe my Los Angeles ghost had followed me to Manhattan the way Jaws followed Ellen Brody from Amity Island to the Bahamas in *Jaws 4: The Revenge* ("This time it's personal"). Maybe the smoke was personal! Maybe it was payback for thinking I could save Sid's soul by selling my house.

Jason was snoring behind the wall of seventeen pillows he used to protect himself from me while he was unconscious.

He claimed he needed the pillows for back support, but I suspect if I'd Sharpied fewer dicks on him in the beginning of our marriage, his back would feel fine. I had stumbled into the bathroom to pee without turning on the lights when I noticed something just outside my window. Across the courtyard in the building adjacent was a woman smoking out her window. Her apartment was one floor beneath mine, and the rings of smoke billowing out of her dragon mouth were rising directly toward me.

"Naomi!" I knocked. I knew she was still awake because I could see the light of her iPad from under the door (where I was lying on my stomach).

Naomi obligatorily cracked opened her door, undoubtedly regretting her decision to move in.

"I found the smoker!" I said, dragging her out of her room and over to the window.

Together we watched as the dragon lady sucked down three cigarettes back to back. Like with Juicy Fruit gum, she kept packing a new stick in the second the previous one had lost its flavor. My stomach turned as I watched each cloud rise from her lips and hit the porous brick surrounding Sid's nursery window.

"What the fuck! This can't be legal! Should I shout at her?"

"No. We must wait," Naomi said, like a trained assassin.

I watched as she took in the scene. But before I could ask another question, she turned and silently walked back to her room.

"So, wait, what do I do?" I trailed after her, trying to get more information, but it was no use. Naomi was done talking. When the time was right, I would be given further instructions, but until then, I had to wait. Naomi disappeared into her bedroom and closed her door, this time locking it.

The next day, Jason's little sister, Veronica, showed up for the weekend. Veronica still lived in Bergen County and made an effort each week to drive into the city to spend time with Sid. Recently, she'd been spending more time with us than usual, due in large part to a dramatic breakup with a one-legged man. She didn't know right off the bat that he had only one leg. It was something that was revealed with time. Veronica pursued the relationship anyway, but things went south when the man became convinced Veronica was humping his stump during sex. After accusing Veronica of having acrotomophilia, or an amputee fetish, the one-legged man threw her out of his house. The relationship ended in a dramatic screaming match on the man's front porch, where he used his fake leg to barricade the front door, prohibiting Veronica from entering.

Hearing her talk, you would never guess that the five-foot-tall Snooki look-alike was in fact a Montessori schoolteacher. Outside of work, she was as refined as Joe Pesci in *Goodfellas*. She screamed, she cursed, she gave people the bird while driving. But Monday through Friday, she headed up the Parent-Teacher Association and was an authority on the rail industry of Sodor Island.

"You know I stopped smoking my menthols nine months ago!" Veronica said, emotionally stuffing her face with a crumb cake she'd sneaked into the apartment while I wasn't looking.

Normally I enjoyed watching others ingest empty calories,

but there was something different about Veronica's urgency. It was as if she knew I was seconds away from snatching the cake out of her hands and jamming my fingers down her throat in a desperate attempt to get her life back on track. Part of Veronica liked having me police her and the other part of her hated me for it. Veronica needed a mommy figure in her life, and when I met Jason, I filled those shoes. After all, I liked having a project. Over the course of seven summers together I'd encouraged Veronica to switch jobs, break up with various (two-legged) boyfriends, and, most recently, to stop smoking. But now that I had an actual kid, my patience with Veronica had run thin and I found myself resenting her for not taking better care of herself and for placing any of that responsibility on me.

"I know it isn't you," I said, charging across the room toward the window, like a mother bear protecting her den. "It's whoever lives in that apartment." I pulled Sid up and bounced him on my hip, hoping to lock eyes with the offender. The smoker across the way was igniting something inside me that I hadn't felt since Jason's ex had written me, telling me to stop posting photos of myself in her old beach caftan. Peeking out the window, my blood boiled with outrage, but also my body tingled with excitement. Some kind of confrontation was in the imminent future.

"Does my brother know about this?" Veronica was accustomed to her brother having no idea what we were up to. She was merely asking so she'd have her story straight. In the past we'd omitted all sorts of details and facts in order to protect Jason from his reality.

Fact. Veronica and I spent every summer obsessing over Jason's ex.

*Detail. I set Jason's ex up on a date with my former acting coach,
then went on the date with them (sadly, not in her beach caftan).*

"Not really," I said. "Naomi and I are gonna walk around
the block to see if we can collect more intel." I pulled a baseball
cap over my head and wedged Sid's swollen baby feet into a
pair of sandals before grabbing my keys and leaving.

"What about me?" Veronica asked, wounded that she'd been
excluded from the caper.

"You're too depressed. I need someone who can focus." I
brushed past her out the door.

The sun was just beginning to set as Naomi, Sid, and I
slowly made our way around the block. Sid had been walking
since his first birthday but still hadn't mastered the art of bending his legs. Instead, he just sort of willed himself forward with
his upper body, leaving his rigid lower half no choice but to follow. He was becoming a person before my eyes. He was sweet
and yet sadistic; his favorite pastime was pretending to run me
over with a car. He showed signs of being an OCD clean freak,
walking behind me, picking up towels and folding them. There
were also signs of him being a total raging disaster, pouring
oatmeal over his head and spinning the dogs around the room
by their heads. He reminded me of all the things I loved about
myself coupled with all the things I hated about Jason. But
like a hot guy who never texts you when he says he's going to,
even his annoying qualities were adorable. He was perfect. And
he was gorgeous. More gorgeous than I ever thought a person
could be. I was humbled every time he cast his eyes on me. I
didn't feel good enough for him. I suspected I never would.

When we approached the smoker's building, Naomi and I

spotted an older man with dark, wavy hair haggling with his dry-cleaning deliveryman out front.

"Excuse me," I interrupted. "Do you live in this building?"

"Umm. Yes?" the man answered with trepidation.

"Oh, good. I was just wondering if I could speak to you for a minute. I live in the building behind you."

The deliveryman counted his cash, then plugged his ears with headphones and pedaled off. Naomi carried Sid as we hiked up the front steps of the building, moving in on the clearly angst-ridden tenant.

"How can I help you?" he asked in a hurried tone. He had an accent that sounded French but not French and wore several chunky sterling chains around his stubbly neck.

"I—well, this is a weird question, but do you smoke or know anyone in your building who does?" I glanced at Naomi for approval. She nodded back.

"Smoke? No," he said firmly.

"Oh, okay. Well, what floor do you live on?"

"I—" The man hesitated. "I live on six. But I have to go now, I have a conference call." He punched a series of numbers into his call box and walked inside without another word.

"Wha—" The door slammed in my face before I could continue. I turned to Naomi, who was grimacing at the door.

"He's lying. I can taste it."

"Really?" I asked.

Nothing made me happier than getting confirmation that somebody was hiding something from me, because it instantly justified my unhealthy need to pry into his or her personal life.

Turning to the call box, I impulsively pushed every button and waited for someone to pick up.

Beep, beep, beep. The call box hummed.

"We're Amazon Prime drones, if anybody answers," I said to Naomi, adjusting my beat-up Ramones tank to make it look more official.

After several seconds, a UPS man appeared. It was Rico, the same UPS guy who delivered to our building.

"Hola. Cómo estás?" Naomi flirted. Rico opened the door and wheeled his hand trolley full of boxes past us.

"Hi, Rico! How's the family?" I smiled eagerly.

Naomi held the door for Rico, then motioned for me to enter behind him.

"Everybody is good, thank you," Rico said, as I awkwardly and uncomfortably adhered to his ass.

Once I was in, I peeled myself off Rico and followed Naomi and Sid into the stairwell. Sid kicked and screamed as we made our way up to the third floor, desperate to negotiate a flight on his own. After spending ten minutes on one step, I decided that not only did Sid's motor skills suck, they were jeopardizing the entire mission. Soon Jason would return home and start asking questions. Stressed for time, I charged ahead, leaving Naomi to handle Sid. The third floor was dark, with worn-down commercial carpet that hadn't been redone since the year I was born. I let my nose guide me through the musky hall until I arrived at apartment 305. Stale tobacco residue permeated the air. Yellow nicotine stains framed the dilapidated door. This was the den of the dragon woman, I was sure. I could hear footsteps inside, but I didn't dare knock.

Minutes later, Sid barreled down the corridor behind me, screaming. Naomi tried to hush him, but it was no use, he'd gone completely rogue. Knowing it was only a matter of time before my rookie ride-along botched the entire operation, I started to panic. I snooped around the neighboring apartments, hoping to catch someone I could turn into an ally. Surely I wasn't the only person affected by the copious amounts of carcinogen affecting their community. But nobody was home. We waited several more minutes before Sid's face turned beet red. Standing at arm's length behind an imaginary wall, he was pooping. He stared straight at me to make sure I wasn't staring at him, as any direct eye contact during one of his bowel movements was strictly forbidden. Once he'd finished, he was back to his fun-loving self and amenable to being held. I threw him over my shoulder and scurried home, hoping I'd beat Jason.

"They're back!" Veronica screamed, before we got through the front door. In the time we'd been gone, she had changed into pajamas, applied five more coats of eyeliner, and confessed everything to her brother.

"I was about to call the cops! What the hell were you doing over there?" Jason stormed out of the bedroom, trying to catch his breath.

Veronica looked at me guiltily. "He promised we could watch *Dateline* if I told him where you were. I'm going through a breakup. I'm weak!"

There was no point in lying. I was too excited not to share what I'd learned.

"We made it into the building! The perp lives in apartment 305." I went online and entered the dragon lady's address to see if I could get her name.

"Jenny, no. I don't want you engaging with our neighbors. We just moved here full-time. This isn't like Los Angeles. We're part of a co-op. We live with other people now, and this is not the way to start our relationship with them. Besides, I have a guy coming tomorrow to spray insulation foam in the brick."

I ignored him, typing frantically. "Baby, it's pollution and it's affecting our lifestyle. Let me at least send a message to our board . . ."

Jason looked at me and shook his head adamantly *no*. "Jenny, if you send a message I am going to be extremely pissed."

"Okay," I said.

Seconds later, I sent a message to the board asking if anybody else was having a problem with the smoke.

Naomi took Sid into his room to change his diaper and break the news that he'd been temporarily fired from the snoop squad until he was potty-trained, had better cardiovascular endurance, and understood the meaning of "inside voice." Veronica checked her text messages by the window, secretly hoping to hear from One Leg.

"There's a guy in there," she said, glancing nonchalantly at apartment 305.

I rushed back over to the window and dropped my laptop in shock.

"NAOMI! It's the guy!"

Standing on the fire escape was the guy with weird man jewelry that we'd met hours earlier.

"He was lying! He said he lived on the sixth floor!"

Naomi smiled a knowing smile. "Told you."

"What is happening to everyone?" Jason interrupted, breaking up the viewing party by drawing the curtains closed.

"What? I can't even wave at them?"

"No! That is the last thing I want you doing." He turned his attention to Naomi. "My wife has a problem and you need to not encourage her," Jason explained soberly, as though I wasn't in the room. Veronica disappeared into Sid's nursery so as not to get a lecture of her own. "She and my sister have a history of bad behavior, and I am hoping that now that she is a mother and role model she will show some restraint when it comes to invading people's personal lives."

"I don't get what the problem is with a simple wave," I huffed to myself. "It's neighborly."

"He just lit up," Veronica blurted out, now watching from Sid's window.

"What? Two smokers!" I ran down the hall to Sid's room.

Unlike his wife, who smoked strictly out the right side of the building, the wavy-haired man was smoking on the left-side fire escape, the fire escape that pointed directly at our bathroom.

I went back to the computer, where I was beginning to yield results. "Their names are Yosi and Esther Soha. They are Israeli Jews from Tel Aviv. She is an artist and he's a jeweler. They've owned the four-bedroom loft since 1983 and tried to sell it last year on some HGTV reality show. Two sons. One cat. Oh, and according to her Facebook, she bought a set of tea towels off Gilt Groupe yesterday."

I talked aloud through the entire *Dateline* episode.

"I am going to be extremely pissed if you try reaching out to them," Jason warned me.

Of course that just made me want to do it more. Jason could bring up something I wasn't even interested in doing and just like that I'd be intrigued. It was Pavlovian.

I stepped away from the computer and paced around the room, trying for once to make a mature decision.

"Jenny! I'm serious." He turned from the couch and scowled.

I watched from the window as Esther sat in front of her computer, checking her e-mail. It would have been so easy to reach out and yet . . . I couldn't. Not this time. I was stuck between being the woman I wanted to be and being the woman I was supposed to be. I wasn't twenty-four anymore. I wasn't even thirty-four. I had to let this go.

The next morning, Naomi and Sid ate pancakes at the table while Veronica sat on the couch, rehashing the last fifteen minutes of her relationship with One Leg.

"He sat in his wheelchair using the fucking leg as a weapon! Who does that? He called me a 'stubby chaser,' you know, instead of a 'chubby chaser,' like I fuckin' set out to date a guy with one leg!"

"You can do better," Naomi said sternly.

"But why does part of me want him back?" Veronica whined.

I bit my tongue, intent on not weighing in. Just then, Jason walked through the front door with the ventilation expert.

"Is everybody decent? We're going to the back room to do some caulking," he announced proudly.

Two more workers appeared behind him and wandered into our bedroom.

"He's cute," Veronica whispered, checking out one of the workers' butts as he walked past.

Jason peeked his head out of the bedroom to notify me that all the open airways in our walls had been sealed, and unless I was knocked up, I wasn't going to smell anything. The ventilation expert showed me the Styrofoam-like substance he used to fill in the gaps. I wasn't dissatisfied with the work. Part of me felt hopeful. But the other part of me still felt like confronting

Esther. If she could see things from my point of view, perhaps she'd be compelled to quit smoking altogether. The expert left an extra can of foam in case I found any forgotten spots before following Jason out.

Once Jason was gone, I ran back over to the window to check on Esther. She was watching the news and drinking coffee. I held Teets's front paws like a puppeteer, forcing him to use only his hind legs to parade back and forth along the windowsill like he was the dog from *Frasier*. I knew I couldn't reach out to Esther directly, but if she were, for instance, convinced that the dog from *Frasier* lived nearby and found herself compelled to wave to him from across the courtyard, I'd have no choice but to crawl out onto my fire escape and start a conversation.

Unnerved by the puppet show happening next to her head, Veronica pulled a blanket up to her chin and closed her eyes.

I dropped Teets and glared at Veronica. "Are you going back to bed? It's the middle of the day!"

"I ate seven pancakes. You know I can't stay awake after I eat. I should have asked for that worker's number . . . It's like on one hand, I'm ready to move on and start dating someone new. But on the other hand—"

"There is no other hand!" I said, finally losing my cool.

"That worker only had one hand?" Veronica's eyes flashed with excitement.

"What? No! Oh my God, you really might be a stubby chaser!"

Veronica looked up at me, suddenly concerned that she had a problem.

To my surprise and slight disappointment, the Styrofoam spray worked. "Thank God you didn't send a crazy letter to the board." Jason sighed every night before bed. Curiously, the board never returned my letter, which I assumed meant they'd read my first book and mutually decided that I was unwell. Days went by and I didn't smell anything. Then late one Saturday night I woke up choking on what smelled like stale smoke. I sprang out of bed and ran to the window to see Esther sucking down a pack of her signature Marlboro reds. With her window shut! I crept out of the bedroom so as not to wake Jason and stormed off to find Veronica and Naomi.

"Guys! It's back! Her window isn't even open and I can smell it!" Veronica's head slowly emerged from a ball of blankets on the couch like a lethargic turtle's.

Naomi opened the door to her bedroom groggily.

Slowly, the three of us made our way toward the window.

"Yup, that's smoke." Veronica yawned. "Maybe I should start smoking again so I at least have a filter to my face when I come over for visits."

I pressed my cheek against the window and noticed several small gaps in the mortar binding her brick unit together.

"This can't go on. I have to do something," I whined, desperate.

Naomi tore her hair out of a gigantic ponytail on the top of her head. The strap on her mildly inappropriate leopard nightgown slunk off her left shoulder as she whipped her long mane of black braids off to one side, ready for a fight.

"Tonight, this ends."

Naomi disappeared into the darkness, then reappeared with the extra can of Styrofoam sealant. She placed the can in my hands without saying a word. I knew what had to be done. Though I was certain this would fall under the umbrella of "Things Jason wouldn't want me doing," I'd run out of options. I'd tried being patient. But patient was giving Sid cancer. It was time to protect my family—and ever so slightly break the law. The Styrofoam sealant had drastically decreased the amount of smoke getting into my bedroom. I saw no real harm in using my spare bottle of foam to do a little touch-up work on the exterior of Esther's unit. The way I saw it, Esther loved smoking, so I was doing her a favor.

"Cigarettes are expensive these days," I reassured myself, as I slipped into one of Jason's ski masks and a pair of flip-flops. "Why should she want to share any of them with me?"

Veronica applied more eyeliner in the event that a mug shot was in her future and followed Naomi and me into the bathroom. Stealthily, I cracked open the window and crawled out onto the fire escape.

"I hope this works," I whispered, my heart racing with adrenaline.

Using the ladder, I wiggled down one flight of stairs to Esther and Yosi's balcony.

Naomi and Veronica hung out the window, watching. Once I was down, Naomi handed me the can of sealant and started pointing out possible cracks. I carefully filled in the holes along Esther's wall.

"Did I ever tell you how he lost his leg?" Veronica called out in a hushed voice.

"How?" I asked, for once appreciating the distraction.

"His neighbor shot him."

"What?" I looked up, nearly tripping on the fire-escape grate.

"I'm just kidding. I think he was born with it."

"Shh!" Naomi smacked Veronica on the head.

"But seriously, do you think we are ever getting back together?"

"No! It's over!" I whispered firmly. "There, I said it. You need to move on." I continued working. "Look at everything Naomi has been through in her life. And do you hear her whining? Until you escape South America—"

Naomi stopped me.

"I'm not from South America."

"You aren't?" I glanced up, confused. "Where are you from?"

"Guatemala."

"That's not South America?"

"No, it's right under Mexico."

"Huh. So you only had to cross two borders to enter the States."

"*Sí,*" she said.

Somehow the idea of Naomi making her way up from Central America was less impressive than picturing her journey from the depths of the Amazon. Even my housekeeper Lita had made it all the way from Bolivia. Maybe I was giving Naomi too much credit. Maybe she wasn't such an authority on guerrilla warfare. Maybe I shouldn't have been hanging off a fire escape with only her and my obsessive sister-in-law supervising. Maybe I needed to work on my geography.

Before I could inquire if Naomi had ever impaled anyone with a machete like she had in my fantasies, a shadow appeared to my right. As I turned, I saw one of Esther's wrinkled hands lift open her window and ash her dying Marlboro into the abyss below. Trying to be still, I sucked in my stomach and held my breath. If she happened to peer over the ledge, our faces would meet. I closed my eyes tightly, trying to think of how I'd explain what I was doing on her fire escape. Could I be doing some neighborly window washing at two in the morning? Or maybe I was trying to make it to ten thousand steps on my Fitbit. Naomi put her hand up, cautioning me to stop moving. Then, as quickly as Esther appeared, she was gone.

I rushed back up the stairs and climbed back in the window, hoping I'd finally solved the issue.

The next day was Sunday. Naomi took off to visit her sister in Brooklyn and Veronica headed back to Jersey. Jason and I spent the day drinking cold-brewed coffee and strolling Sid around the city. I'd felt so accomplished and at peace as I went back to bed the night before, but this morning as we were getting ready to leave the house, I found myself riddled with doubt. *Was I smelling smoke again?* I'd become so obsessed that I couldn't even say for sure anymore.

I was sitting on a park bench watching Jason swing Sid and replaying last night's events when an e-mail popped up on my phone. It was from our co-op board, and they'd cc'd Jason.

Dear Jenny, we got your e-mail about the smoke problem and didn't want to write back until we checked with our lawyers about whether or not we had any jurisdiction over the communal corridor. Sadly, there's not much we can do about someone else's building. The only thing we might suggest is reaching out and asking them to stop.

I quickly waved at Jason to solidify our marriage before scouring the area for his phone. I needed to delete the e-mail from the co-op before Jason yelled at me for reaching out. But it was no use, Jason's phone glared at me from his back pocket. The e-mail from the co-op was waiting patiently in his in-box.

If Jason learned that I'd acted against his wishes and written to the co-op board, he'd know that I hadn't let the whole thing go—that I was still plagued by the neighbors' smoke. He'd never let me anywhere near their building. I had to do something quick. It was like I'd already ruined my diet for the day by eating a loaf of bread, so I might as well build myself an ice-cream sundae out of everything else in my pantry.

I'll start abstaining from neighbors tomorrow, I assured myself.

"Baby, I have to go home, I'm bleeding!" I called out to Jason, using the oldest excuse in the book.

Jason looked at me from across the playground, mortified.

I delicately sauntered out of the park, explaining that I'd meet him back at the apartment. Instead of heading home, however, I ran directly to Esther and Yosi's. If I was going to talk to Esther I had to act fast, before Jason had a chance to read his e-mail and guess where I was headed. After all, it wasn't my idea anymore. I was merely following my co-op board's suggestion.

Beep, beep, beep.

The buzzer rang three times before a woman answered.

"Hello, I'm from next door. I was hoping I could talk to you," I stuttered nervously.

The door opened and I headed inside, unprepared for what was to come.

When I reached the third floor, Esther was waiting for me.

Her face was older than I expected, a stark contrast to the spiky gray Mohawk and wooden tribal earplugs I'd noticed from my window. She wore platform Doc Martens, a flowing purple skirt, and a colorful cotton shirt emblazoned with a screen print of Ganesh, the Indian elephant god of transitions. Her look was half punk rock, half yoga studio gift shop. She seemed like the type of person who'd shared needles with Basquiat in the eighties and had tantric sex with Sting in the nineties.

"Hello, I'm Esther and this is my husband, Yosi," she said, inviting me inside.

Yosi looked at me guiltily. He tried to stay composed, knowing he'd been completely busted for lying to me about living on the sixth floor.

The loft looked exactly the way it did on HGTV, only messier. A large Buddha statue sat on a coffee table littered with magazines and empty Marlboro cartons.

"Please sit." Yosi gestured toward a large chair adorned with cat hair and fancy silk pillows.

"I'm actually allergic to cats," I confessed, already getting off on a bad foot.

I walked over to the cracked window, desperate for some fresh air, and propped myself on the ledge.

"Okay. So how can we help you?" Yosi stared at me blankly.

I thought about where to start. "So . . . I just moved here from Los Angeles and I haven't lived in an apartment in many years. I obviously did when I was younger and never had any problems with my neighbors." I waited for Esther to say something, but she just continued to stare. "Okay, I actually might have broken my lease once in my twenties because I slept with the guy upstairs, but other than that, it's been smooth sailing."

"Very good," Yosi chimed in awkwardly.

"The point is, your smoking is coming into my apartment and hurting my baby."

Several seconds passed as Esther and Yosi translated what I'd just said in their heads. Finally, Esther spoke.

"You moved into Manhattan with a baby? Aren't people usually leaving the city with babies?"

"Well, if you must know, I was trying to get away from a ghost, but there's a small chance he might have followed me . . . The point is, until you stop smoking into my apartment I'm not really going to know where my real problems lie, because right now, all I can focus on is the air quality." My voice cracked with desperation.

"And you couldn't just e-mail?" Esther looked at Yosi, then back at me.

"I suggested that! But my husband told me I was being immature." I gloated like a middle child who'd just won a debate at the dinner table.

"Well, Yosi only smokes weed. The cigarettes are all me," Esther confessed. "I wish I could tell you I'd quit. I did for twenty years. But ever since my youngest son left for the Israeli Army, I've been back at it. Do you have any idea how scary it feels as a mother to let your baby leave home?"

I could feel my heart accelerating. The idea of Sid leaving me was perhaps the most gut-wrenching thought I could imagine. Whether I wanted to admit it or not, that's how this was all going to end. Maybe he wasn't going to run off to Israel, but eventually he was going to want to go somewhere—anywhere I wasn't. Unexpected tears streamed down my cheeks.

"It's just so terrifying. You feel out of control. Like there is nothing in your power you can do to protect the one thing you are on this planet to look after." Esther strung her words together slowly and eloquently as Yosi nodded and rolled a blunt.

"I know! It's horrible."

"I wish I could tell you it gets easier. But it does not. It gets harder. And you love harder. And it hurts . . . And then you die . . . The cigarettes are bad. They are terrible, but I'm just smoking because I can't do anything else." Esther shook her head, disappointed with herself.

Yosi finished rolling his blunt and held it neatly between his fingers.

I took a deep breath, then turned to Yosi, overcome with emotion.

"I think I need a hit of that."

As much as I'd demonized Esther, I couldn't avoid relating to her. As mothers, we shared the same anxieties. I wished we'd shared the same allergies, but maybe that was asking too much. I hated her smoking, and I'd told her as much, but at the end of the day, I couldn't control how she lived her life. I could hardly control my own. Esther was sympathetic to my situation and vowed to smoke strictly off her front patio, killing the Chinese couple in the building to our left instead. For the time being, that was going to have to do.

I released a deep, smoky sigh of relief and cast my bloodshot eyes up to my apartment.

Staring back at me, through the large picture window, was Jason, his eyes squinted as if he didn't believe what he was seeing. The cloud from my hit made it look like there was smoke coming out of his ears as he stood there, dumbfounded. There was nothing left to do but wave.

7
HELL IS OTHER PEOPLE'S CHILDREN

I kind of want to have a girl go down on me while I blow you." I batted my eyes at Jason across the table, trying to spice up an overly planned date night. A skinny hipster in suspenders placed two menus in front of us and disappeared into the bustling bistro without a second glance.

Jason picked up his menu and studied it like he was reading the Torah. "If we do the lottery for Washington Market, it still doesn't guarantee we'll even get an application. Don't you have any mom friends you can ask? What do they say about Avenues?"

Before I had time to throw an artisanal breadstick at his head, the waiter reappeared to take our drink orders. Jason looked at me, then at the waiter.

"Can you tell your bartender to make me a fun mocktail? Something fizzy?"

I stared at the waiter, who was at least a decade younger than me. It bothered me that people that young were old enough to join the workforce, and that girls born in 1997 were eighteen now, and that the guy who first introduced me to cocaine only drank mocktails.

It wasn't Jason's sobriety that annoyed me, it's what it represented. The party was over. It was time to be responsible—to start brushing my hair before I left the house, to take vitamins, to use dental floss, to listen to my voicemail, to write thank-you notes, to make holiday cards, to develop crow's-feet, and to stop having sex with other people.

"Baby. What the fuck? I just said I wanted to have another threesome. Aren't sober guys supposed to turn into sex addicts? Don't you at least want to fuck my head through a wall?"

The truth was a threesome sounded exhausting. But at the very least it was something exciting to talk about. It's important in long-term relationships to have common interests that aren't just pedicures and documentaries on farm-to-table cooking.

"Sure, yes, I wanna fuck you through a wall." Jason yawned, sipping his Safe Sex on the Beach. "But I also wanna get Sid into the best nursery school. You need moms in your life that can give us these answers."

"Jason, I've *never* had a mom in my life with answers."

"Well, start looking."

In concept, I understood that there were cool moms in the world just waiting to be discovered, but for some reason I couldn't seem to attract any. Every time I tried to put myself out there at a Mommy and Me, confessing to the cutest-dressed girl in the room that I hated the other fifteen women sitting around us, she would inevitably turn on me and, when I left her side, would tell the rest of the group all the horrible things

I was saying about them. When it came to the mom world, I feared I'd always be a fish out of water, and Jason a fish out of vodka.

I needed to find a mom like me who loved her child but also found time to work, work out, and post cute pics of herself on the Internet. I wanted someone who hated authority, who loved books (preferably mine), who didn't use the "praise God" hands emoji, and who understood that the movie *Clue* was one of the greatest films of American cinema. She should be about two years older than me, slightly less cute, ideally ten pounds heavier. She should wear a size-eight shoe, have exquisite taste in clothes, live and work in my neighborhood, have an office with a printer that I could use, be able to take long lunch breaks, and know how to do makeup.

Why was this woman so hard to find?

I explained this very patiently to Jason as he gnawed the leg off his brioche-stuffed chicken.

"That's a lot to ask for," he said, laughing at me. "How about you first just find someone who speaks English."

He had a point. Not having the confidence to approach other moms in TriBeCa, I'd taken to befriending their nannies. I had a list of names in my phone that I couldn't pronounce and at least a dozen playdates I'd committed to without realizing. My friend Gretchen had two older kids she'd raised in the city and suggested I join a group called Hudson River Mamas, but just the name annoyed me. I pictured the members wearing matching leather jackets with their last names embroidered on the back. They probably spent their days trolling the local playgrounds looking to fight other mom groups who'd made the mistake of wandering down from Chelsea. According to their website, the application process required a letter of recommendation and an in-person interview, where I was certain I'd be asked to choose my favorite Honest Diaper pattern. (The anchors.)

There was no world in which I was going to join a club to make friends. The idea was downright insulting. I was a successful, fun-loving free spirit (with a famous husband that I can force to emcee your kid's Bar Mitzvah). Women should have been clamoring to hang out with me. But alas, they weren't. The one girlfriend I had living in my area was the one girlfriend I'd always had.

⸺

Even though she was just as boy-crazy as my mom, I'd always felt safe with Crystal Fontaine. That was because I knew all of her relationships were doomed from the start. Though she was always claiming that this time she'd found a good guy, Crystal never liked anyone who liked her back. She was in a constant state of waiting the requisite two days after sleeping with someone to see if she was ever going to hear from them again. And she always did. But only so they could sleep with her again and then go back to never calling her. Crystal didn't believe in confrontation. She preferred to end her relationships by firing off a series of psychotic texts and then throwing her phone into the back of a cab and watching it disappear along with her entire contact list. "I needed a new phone anyway," she'd claim.

I'd met Crystal when we were kids and had managed to stay in her life because I, too, was a self-involved, unavailable asshole who could never completely commit. I kept her at arm's length, where I kept most women. But unlike most women, Crystal loved the distance. I was drawn to Crystal because she was smarter than she wanted to be, funnier than she realized, and because trying to fix her obsession with men allowed me to pretend I was actually fixing my mother's.

When Crystal wasn't busy flirting with dirty clubrats, she flirted with the idea of one day moving to Manhattan. She worked in fashion magazines and New York City was indisputably the epicenter of her industry. Eight months earlier I'd encouraged her to pack up her life in Manhattan Beach and follow her dream. I forget if I was mad at her or just exhausted, but for whatever reason I was compelled to tell her that she was going to end up getting gang-banged on a pinball machine unless she left town fast. I knew Jason, Sid, and I would be relocating to New York for a few months for Jason's play, and I thought it'd be fun to have a friend I could drag with me to Century 21 while he was busy working. But it occurred to me that at the end of those few months, we'd fly back to our life in Los Angeles and Crystal Fontaine would be left on her own in Gotham City. Deep down I didn't want to part with Crystal. But just like her relationships with men, I never really took any of her plans seriously. I assumed she'd try out the East Coast for about as long as I was there, then follow me back to Los Angeles, bitching about how she hated cold weather and ethnic guys. Surprisingly, however, Crystal committed to her new life in the city wholeheartedly. She'd snuggled into a small walk-up in Greenwich Village and had become the mayor of her block on Foursquare.

"I'm never going back. I hate Los Angeles!" Crystal whipped back her platinum-blond bob and wagged her finger "no" into the brisk September air. With an overly confident sashay and a bubble butt filled with silicone, she looked like the Kim Kardashian emoji you'd send your sorority sisters when you finalized your divorce.

"Help peas, help peas . . ." Sid said, struggling to break free from his stroller. I pushed him along the boardwalk to the park as Crystal followed, stalking herself on Facebook.

"*Nien, Kinder.* Sit back, please," I said, like I was giving a command to one of the dogs.

"I sent this to Princeton last night." Crystal looked at me diabolically, then flashed me a full-frontal shot of herself lying in bed. Crystal never called anyone she was involved with by his name; it made her feel too vulnerable. She preferred instead to give each player in her life an alias. So if White Tank Top, for example, suddenly got back together with his girlfriend, it was no big deal. If she accidentally drunk-texted Black Dildo, she'd live. In Crystal's mind, the only way to stay immune to heartbreak was to never humanize anyone. She claimed she was open to the idea of love—but so does everybody who's actually trying to avoid it. Crystal didn't love herself; there was no way she was going to accept the love of a Black Dildo.

"He replied saying that I was the nicest person he's ever met. What do you think that means?" Crystal asked in a tone that said "Lie to me or I will cut you out of my life indefinitely."

"That he's not into you," I said bluntly.

By the time we'd reached the park, Sid's upper body was completely free from his seat belt and Crystal was giving me the silent treatment. I tipped Sid's stroller toward me, sending him backward into his seat, before opening the wrought-iron gate and rolling inside. Children of all ages flew around the rubber-surfaced playground like kamikaze pilots. Hunched-over schoolmarms doled out handfuls of animal crackers from giant Costco tubs to a line of toddlers strung together on a walking rope like chubby paper dolls. A herd of older moms in wedge sneakers and diamond studs bigger than their ear-lobes huddled together in the shade with their iced soy lattes, whispering about their Hamptons homes and the accidental orgasms they were having in SoulCycle. On the far side of the park sat a row of Jamaican nannies texting on their cell phones, comparing salaries and paid vacation days.

"But he's the one who wrote me immediately after our date thanking me for a lovely time. That was very sweet!" Crystal was unable to let the Princeton thing go.

"Why are we rewarding people for being normal?" I asked, distracted.

My ears perked up when an androgynous mom with no boobs and intentionally distressed jeans walked past, holding hands with a little boy in checkered Vans. I don't like to judge a book by its cover, but I do believe in judging a kid based on how hot his mom is. Sadly, No Boobs's kid looked about five, too old for Sid. I'd learned early on not to hit on a potential mom friend unless our kids were in the *exact* same develop-mental place. In the first twelve to twenty-four months of your kid's life, every week makes a difference. So if, for instance, I tried to start a conversation with the mom of a three-year-old, she might be polite and give me her number, but what she'd really be thinking was *Get the fuck away from me, you don't know my life.* Our kids would have nothing in common. Her child was able to form complete sentences. Sid was still calling Jason "Mommy" and shitting on the bathroom floor.

I helped Sid down from his stroller and sidled up next to a girl in sweatpants pushing a two-year-old John Candy look-alike on the swings.

"How old is he?" I asked, trying to make conversation.

The girl looked at me like I was a pedophile who'd just offered her son a pack of Starburst before answering curtly, "He's a she."

"Mo, mo, mo," Sid said, demanding that I push him higher.

I turned to Crystal, who was scoping out a silver-haired banker drowning in the sandbox with his son. His eyes glazed over, daydreaming about his life one month prior when school wasn't back in session and his wife was living full-time in Bridgehampton.

"What is everyone's problem here?" I shook my head, flummoxed.

"This park sucks. There are no hot dads." Still furious that I wasn't being a good enough friend to let her drive her life off a cliff, Crystal got back on her phone, refusing to make eye contact. "Have you heard of Raya?"

"Is it a place I can meet cool moms?"

"It's like Tinder for hot people. Like, you have to be super-hot to be accepted . . . or Matthew Perry. We have plans." She smirked proudly. "Remember when I was on that site Beautiful People and I met the Gyno?"

"Wait, that's your code name for him?"

"No. This guy really is my gyno. He's a smokehouse . . . and he has a big dick."

"How do you know that?" I looked at her, concerned.

"It's unimportant. Anyway, online is basically the only way I date. I've given up trying to meet people in the real world.

I just don't trust someone when I don't know right off the bat what mutual friends we have. It's creepy."

Maybe Crystal was right. Maybe meeting people face-to-face was passé. But everyone I was friends with online was either a stranger or a celebrity French bulldog. Waylaid by a new prospect, Crystal forgot why she was mad at me and again started showing me pictures of her tits.

I looked back over at the mom in sweatpants, who was now packing up her things and stuffing John Candy into a thin, gauzy sling across her chest. Despite my best efforts to exude confidence and congeniality, I was being overlooked on the playground, the way I'd been my whole life. I'd always suspected the dearth of girlfriends in my childhood was a result of being the new girl in school or my dad buying me clothes from T.J.Maxx, but I wasn't any newer to parenthood than a lot of these bitches. Yes, my linen shirt might have been covered in holes, but I still overpaid for it at Fred Segal. *What was I doing wrong?*

That night, Jason and I did what all couples do once their kids are in bed: we stopped speaking and stared at our iPads. After a half hour of silence, I made an announcement.

"Well, I just joined Tinder."

Jason turned to look at me, at last noticing that I'd camouflaged my acne in a thick coat of Sid's diaper-rash cream.

"Jenny, I'm not having a threesome with some weirdo off Tinder." He paused for a minute trying to make sense of my DIY Kabuki makeup. "Unless she's hot."

"I'm over the threesome idea," I said, applying more cream.

"How do you always get over the threesome idea before I even get a chance to act on it?" he whined. "It's not fair."

"Because, Jason, I'm a mother now. I'm too tired for threesomes. Unless it's me with two people that aren't you."

Jason gasped with mock horror, then went back to his iPad. We'd been together long enough that it was no longer offensive to joke about the downsides of monogamy.

"Besides, I'm not joining Tinder to find hot chicks," I clarified. "I'm joining to find hot moms."

"Wow. That's sad." Jason raised his leg above his head like a dancer and farted as loudly as his body would allow. The noise reverberated off the sheets and sent Gina flying across the room like she was escaping an air strike in Baghdad. Jason smiled at me, waiting for my reaction. Knowing it would give him far too much satisfaction, I ignored him.

"I might have just pooped," he said, still hoping to get a rise out of me.

" 'Super-queer cuddle switch with a strong tendency toward big spoon,' " I read aloud. I held up a picture of a large butch black woman in a neon crop top. "But what's a cuddle switch?"

Jason shrugged and swiped to the next picture.

For the next two hours we fell into a Tinder K-hole.

"What about Connie? She seems normal? She's a wanderer, a reader, and a runner," I said.

"Okay. Swipe right."

"Diane could be fun. But her profile picture is just a close-up of one eye."

"That means she's fat," Jason explained.

Before we could continue, a notification popped up on the

screen. We'd swiped too many profiles and were being suspended from "playing" for the next six hours.

"Boo!" Jason flopped back down on his side of the bed. "Should I start an account?"

"No!" I said.

"Why not? I should get to if you are." Though Jason often found himself playing the Desi to my Lucy, the truth was that he preferred being an Ethel. Yes, he was a rule dork, the type of guy who if he saw a line would immediately get in it, the type of know-it-all who would have gotten stabbed at my high school for not letting anyone cheat off his midterm. But there was another side to him, the freewheeling lunatic. The kind of guy who, if encouraged, would ask a Costa Rican cabbie for weed, eat street meat in Shanghai, or pay money to bungee jump off a rusty crane in Tijuana. He was impulsive and adventurous in all the ways I wasn't. (Mainly the ways that lead to hospitalization and/or concussions.) He got a thrill out of life in the fast lane, so long as I made a convincing argument for why we needed to carpool illegally. In our early years, my harebrained ideas coupled with his joie de vivre had led to ill-advised tattoos, third-world urgent-care centers, and our almost going to prison in Turkey. But now we were parents, and we couldn't afford to take the same kinds of risks. One of us had to be the designated driver—at least until Sid was old enough to see over the dashboard.

"Besides," he continued, "I'm much better with women than you are." Shopping for girlfriends was precisely the type of shenanigan that Jason loved. Not only did it give him an excuse to perform, but it also allowed him to compete with me. Aside from when it came to Sid, or our dogs, our therapist, our couples friends, or our dry cleaner Nick, I avoided competing with Jason, because it only made me frustrated when he won. And annoyingly, he nearly always won. He was faster, stronger, and able to answer almost any *Jeopardy!* question, or at least the ones they put in the backs of New York City cabs.

I'm therapized enough to admit that my need to outdo Jason (and every man I've ever met) is the direct result of having been raised by my first husband, otherwise known as my dad, who encouraged me to do great things, but mainly so they'd reflect well on him. He allowed me victories, money, and attention, just so long as *he* always had more. When you grow up waiting in the wings, watching your dad-husband soak in a particular kind of spotlight, it's hard not to resent a legitimately famous person.

When I first met Jason, I instantly rooted for his demise. Not because I didn't like him; I didn't even know him. What I didn't like was that he was successful and famous and I wasn't. It triggered me. Before meeting him for the first time, a producer friend (who was trying to get in good with me so he could fuck my sister) had sent me a password so I could watch all the audition footage for a movie I was up for. I was only supposed to watch the tapes that pertained to my role, but after spending two hours trying to decide who would win in a fight between Lauren German's face and Lake Bell's boobs, I stumbled upon the two guys they were looking at for the lead. One was Joe Schmostein and one was Jason Biggs.

"Fuck Jason Biggs," I said to the producer, having never met him or seen any of his films.

"Really?" he replied. "Did you see his audition?"

"I don't need to. I already think the other guy is better." I had to root for the underdog, I *was* the underdog. And in a weird, Freudian way, Jason Biggs was my dad. (Please forget you ever read that.)

Eventually, my friend asked me to watch Jason's tape, and to my surprise, he was outstanding. He literally blew me away. And somehow, through my desktop Dell, he made me fall in love with him. I told my friend as much, and within several days we were set up on a blind date. The rest is history—and by history, I mean in my first book.

Even though I love my husband and consider him the greatest thing to ever happen to me before Sid and after Teets, it still irks me when I am brushed to the side as people clamor to talk to him. It's not that I'm not proud of him or grateful for his success. It's that the last thing I need in my life is to feel eclipsed by another fucking man. Sure, I'm partly to blame for being attracted to successful people, but there is no denying that being around them tends to ignite a certain unhealthy resentment in me.

This is why I didn't want Jason making a Tinder profile. Because I knew if he did, he'd probably have more mom friends than me. And that could not happen. Unlike my goal of dying with more Twitter followers than Jason, having more mom friends was something within my reach. It was something I knew I could do quickly, without great effort, and without showing my vagina. Or so I thought.

"Why am I not getting any matches? Do you think I need to show my vagina?" I said. I took Jason's phone out of his hand and hid it on my side of the bed. "Baby, I'm the mom. We're focused on me right now."

Jason looked at my profile picture, a publicity shot of David Bowie juggling three crystal orbs from the movie *Labyrinth*.

"Jareth the Goblin King?"

"What? Bowie is awesome," I said, defensive.

"Doesn't he steal children?"

"I—" I didn't have a great response, so I deflected by bursting into song. *"Dance magic dance!"*

Jason could see how desperate I was, and so, like a true gentleman (who knows he is secretly better than you), he allowed Tinder to be strictly my thing.

For the next few days, I checked my matches every chance I got. But nobody seemed to want anything real. Two women started conversations with me, but they never went anywhere. After several quips like "Hiya," "Psst," and "You bi?" the correspondence would abruptly stop. After a while I started to realize that Tinder wasn't about meeting people, it was actually just another way to avoid meeting people. If you can hide behind your phone and get your ego massaged by knowing people want to date you, what's the point of leaving your house to physically engage with them? Even if it's casual sex you're after, after a few tries, the idea quickly becomes hotter than the act itself. The act is messy and awkward and requires someone knowing you're ten years older than your profile pic. Having an ongoing texting relationship with a handful of strangers offers all of the intrigue of a budding romance with none of the disappointment. Frustrated at work? Fire off a "Hiya." Get in a fight with your parents? Throw out a "What's up?" Break up with your real-life girlfriend? "Drinks soon?" Instantly, you are back in the game and feeling strong. I didn't need Tinder for validation; I already used Twitter for that. What I needed was a real-life woman who wasn't all talk and was willing to put out or, at the very least, offer a nursery-school recommendation.

"I think you just need some moral support," Jason said one Sunday after watching me throw my phone across the room. "If you want, I'll go with you to the park and just root from the sidelines. I've been seeing some cute moms up at Bleecker Street."

Jason's work schedule had recently opened up, giving him free time during the week to hang with Sid and be depressed about his work schedule opening up. Jason was the kind of dad that every mom dreams of. He knew his kid's diaper size, shoe size, what buzzwords got him in and out of the bath. While I spent my mornings writing about how my parents ignored me, Jason focused his attention on Sid. They read books, popped bottles, and like all men, eventually settled in front of the TV. Their eyes as big as saucers, their bodies completely still, I could never tell who was enjoying himself more. When we were alone Jason would give me the abridged version of whatever cartoon they'd seen and what major facts I needed to know:

1. The Cookie Monster's real name is Sid;
2. Dora the Explorer is a drug mule;
3. Caillou is going through chemo.

"Part of the problem is that I work and most of these moms don't," I announced arrogantly, as we rolled into the park with Sid that afternoon. The truth is that I felt superior for having a life outside of my husband—but also inferior for having a life outside of my son. I was torn between feeling too good and feeling not good enough.

For all the friendship game I talked, I feared relationships as much as Crystal did. Having mom friends meant trusting women. And trusting women meant opening myself up to heartbreak. Women were scary, dangerous, and always one step away from dropping me for a man. (Or at least my mom was. And so would Crystal, as soon as someone texted her back.) I pushed Pause on my wallowing for long enough to wonder whether moms were avoiding me or I was avoiding moms.

I looked around at the weekend crowd, composed of hungover dads playing on their Apple Watches, helicopter moms cautioning their kids about the dangers of Razor scooters, and random singles wondering why they agreed to brunch with their married friends. Despite our differences, we were all a mess, all trying to survive. Though it could be painful, I knew I had to jump in for Sid's sake. I didn't want him to be excluded from sleepovers and playdates because I was too aloof and hard to make plans with. I couldn't be a loner just because it somehow made me feel special. Whether I worked or not, I was exactly like these women in that I was a new mom. And I refused to stay so closed off that the only kind of female validation I was comfortable receiving was the occasional Tinder text reading "Did you fall from heaven because fuck me." Sucking up my pride and sucking in my stomach, I approached a rattled redhead trying to lift her tantruming toddler off a bike.

"Do you come here often?"

She looked up at me, then rolled her eyes toward her devil daughter. "Sorry, we're missing naptime and about to melt down."

Jason leaned against a picnic table, watching me and shaking his head.

I walked back over to him for feedback.

"Baby, no. You can't just jump in like that. You seem too eager and weird."

"Well, what do I do?"

"Think of it like picking someone up at a bar. First, decide which girl you're interested in. Then talk to everybody but her. Make her come to you. Say some biting things that she happens to overhear. Maybe tell a story that you feel she might relate to." I was suddenly Neil Strauss and Jason was Mystery. I gave him a look, completely weirded out.

"What the fuck, baby? Now I'm just some kind of lounge lizard—" I stopped, seeing an edgy mom with ombré hair. "I should have worn cuter shoes. I'm not peacocking enough!"

"Your shoes are fine."

"I look like a militant lesbian."

"You always look like a militant lesbian. You have penis envy and you're afraid of your own sexuality. Now go track down that kid and position Sid next to it." Jason massaged my neck like I was a boxer about to get in the ring.

Sid looked at me and instantly turned stiff as a board, making it nearly impossible to lift him. It was as if he was aware of my plan and didn't appreciate being used as bait. When I finally got close to Ombré's kid, a pudgy blond Aryan Youth candidate in a "Will work for sugar" T-shirt, Sid was flailing in my arms, crying. After clawing me across the face didn't work, he decided to bite my ear. I reflexively let go of my Kid Dynamite, dropping him on his diaper directly on top of Ombré's kid.

"Bunny! Biting is not allowed!" I shrieked.

"Dylan? You playing nice?"

I turned to see Ombré mom approaching. She was beautiful

in a plain French-person way. She wore a gold wedding band, minimal makeup, an oversize sweater, and cropped jeans. On her ankle I noted a Japanese character tattoo, informing me she'd spent 1999 making the same mistakes I had. Sid looked up at Ombré, unimpressed by her heavy roots and clearly judging her for being stuck in 2007. Dylan, who was several weeks younger than Sid and didn't yet possess the vocabulary to say the word "balayage," stared vacantly at his mother.

"I'm Ulrika. But my friends call me Ricki."

"I'm Jenny. I don't have any friends."

Ombré laughed and sat down on a bench beside me. "I hate this park. I always feel like I'm in that Sartre play *No Exit*," she said.

"I played Inez in *No Exit* in college!" I said excitedly, as if I was telling someone I'd won an Oscar for *The Color Purple*.

Ombré swept her calico locks to the side and looked around. "There's no escaping because we are in New York and what the fuck else are we gonna do with our kids? Let them play on the subway? Have you been to the park on Sullivan Street in SoHo? It's way better."

"No, but my husband probably has." I pointed at Jason, who was hiding behind a tree like a TV vampire that's impervious to sunlight as long as he's wearing a black leather jacket and sunglasses.

Ombré held up her hand to say hello.

"We should go sometime. What time does he nap?"

"Afternoons." I looked to Sid to make sure he noticed that I'd answered the question correctly. "I work during the week, but maybe next weekend?"

"Perfect."

Sid stabbed himself in the mouth with a shovel, officially becoming that belligerent drunk friend who gets you thrown off your Southwest flight to Vegas.

"Give me your number." Ombré took out her phone and typed in my digits as Jason rushed over to honor Sid's feelings, liked he'd read in one of his child development books.

"I can see that you're frustrated about not being able to fit the shovel in your mouth. I get frustrated when I can't do something, too. Let's calm our bodies and figure this out together."

"I'll text you." Ombré winked and walked off.

Jason continued negotiating with a still-convulsing Sid. "Do you want to calm your body now or five minutes from now?"

"Looking forward to it!" I waved.

⟋

"So, like, when do you think she'll text?" I sat on the couch next to Crystal, replaying the day's events. "She seemed into me, right, babe?"

"Totally into you, baby," Jason called out, his body half in the freezer as he sated his sober sweet tooth with spoonfuls of butter-pecan ice cream.

"Wow. Slow down. It's been like three hours. She'll probably text you in a few days." Crystal sounded more levelheaded than I'd ever heard her.

"But this is different. We were exchanging info. We made a tentative plan to go to that park on Sullivan Street. She should have texted her details right away. Maybe the text didn't go through or she forgot or—"

"Or maybe she's just not that into you," Crystal offered

sadistically, for once not the girl having the meltdown. "I think White Tank Top fingered me in that park," she added, before slinking back into her cell.

"Just breathe. You'll hear from her," Jason mumbled through a full mouth of whatever other shit he'd foraged out of the freezer.

Like White Tank Top, Black Dildo, and all the other players who'd come before, Ombré was either going to text or not, and there was nothing I could do to change it. But with each day that passed, I felt more and more hurt. Every time I thought about going to our usual park, I fumed. I'd always used romantic disappointments to my advantage in the past. Even now I'd still sometimes pick a fight with Jason just so I'd be depressed for a week and have an excuse to eat a Benadryl for dinner. So I spent the week combating my feeling of rejection from Ombré by getting my eyebrows waxed, creating an Adele playlist on Spotify, and setting the treadmill to 7.5.

When Sunday finally rolled around, I was ready to move on—partly because Ombré and I didn't have enough history to hold on to and partly because I had a really important meeting on Monday that could potentially lead to me being pasted on a billboard outside Ombré's apartment. Then, like all assholes, the minute I stopped caring she surfaced.

"Hi, Jenny. We still doing the park on Sullivan?" The number wasn't saved in my phone, but I knew exactly who the text was from.

"Ricki?" I wrote, as if it could be any number of other potential mom friends.

"Yeah," she replied. "Are we meeting or what?"

Sandwiched between two buildings was Sullivan Street Park. It was more urban than the other parks in the area. Used push toys and empty Mum-Mum wrappers littered the blacktop basketball court. Popsicle-stained children scrambled around the worn-down jungle gym.

The second we arrived Sid leaped out of his stroller and fought his way into the madness like a newly engaged girl at a David's Bridal sale. His body tightened with excitement as he grunted his way up the spiral slide.

"Jenny!" Ombré said, appearing behind me looking happy and blissfully unaware of our breakup. "Work was crazy this week. How about you?"

"Yeah. Crazy," I said, playing it cool.

After a few minutes of small talk, it occurred to me that I hadn't seen Ombré's son yet. "Where's Dylan?" I finally asked.

"Oh, I didn't want to wake him. He was still napping. But I brought my older son, Forrest." Ombré turned and pointed to a lanky, dark-haired ten-year-old swinging on the monkey bars. We might have been making the same mistakes in '99, but our paths clearly diverged in '06.

"Oh, wow."

"Different dads. Obviously . . . Forrest, get down here!" she seethed, then turned to me, instantly a different person. "God, I've been going all day. Do you mind if I go grab a slice next door? Can you keep an eye on him for a minute?"

"Umm."

"You hungry? Want a Coke?" she asked. "Forrest, be good! I'm getting you a sausage and pepperoni!" And with that she exited the park.

As soon as Ombré was out of sight I called Jason. He answered and immediately started talking.

"Hey, baby! I'm at Whole Foods. Do we need more wipes? The wipes here suck. Anyway, I think I'm gonna make my organic raisin chicken tonight or, I don't know, should I make the cacciatore? It's organic, too. I'm only buying organic now."

"Either one. But, baby? I'm at the park and my date just left me with her kid."

"What do you mean left you?" Jason strained to hear me over two dueling conversations, one about ethical consumerism and the other about brushing your teeth with coconut oil.

"Ombré said she was hungry, so she walked across the street to get pizza. Is that normal?"

"Umm . . ." Jason paused, knowing it wasn't normal. "Yeah, baby. It's fine. She'll be right back, I'm sure."

I looked up and saw Forrest heave one of the broken push toys over his head and clock another child in the face.

"Forrest! No!" I screamed.

"Baby? *Jen?*"

I hung up the phone abruptly and ran to Forrest. Using all the tactics I'd seen Jason perfect on Sid, I took a deep breath and started in.

"Forrest, I see that you are upset that your mom left you at the park. I used to get upset when my mom left me with strangers, too. Let's calm our bodies and figure this out together."

Forrest glared at me for a good ten seconds before speaking. "Suck my dick."

I pulled back, speechless, as he took off running in the opposite direction.

"I'm supposed to be watching you!" I called after him. "You need to stay in this general area, please! Would you like to stay in this general area now or five seconds from now?" Forrest zigzagged around the park like a demented Roadrunner. Parents looked at me and shook their heads disapprovingly. Sid burst into spontaneous laughter, like a person pretending to get a joke he didn't understand. I couldn't help but soften for a moment, appreciating the absurdity of the situation. I walked toward the park's entrance with Sid's giggling body in my arms. Craning my neck out the gate, I saw pizza parlors in both directions. There was no way of knowing which way Ombré had gone. A steady stream of families rotated in and out of the gate as I stood with Sid, waiting for Ombré. I called her cell five times in a row, but it kept sending me straight to voicemail. I texted her a series of question marks, but nothing. I was growing weary and Sid was nodding off, ready for his afternoon nap. The sun beat down overhead, turning September back into the dead of August. Losing hope, I again called Jason.

"She's not coming back." My arms were hot and sticky against Sid's flaccid body.

"How long has it been?"

"I don't know, it feels like two years, but it's probably been closer to forty-five minutes." I tried to wipe the sweat off Sid's porcelain forehead with my sleeve. "Are we concerned at all about global warming or do we just care that Sid is eating organic?"

Jason ignored my question and cut to the chase.

"Where's the kid, Jenny?"

"I don't even care anymore," I said, defeated.

"Jenny! Don't say that. Can you see him?"

"Yes, yes, he's loading the slide up with dirt so nobody can use it, it's fine." I was over caring about Forrest. "I gotta get Sid out of here. The sun exposure alone feels like child abuse." I looked up at the brick buildings boxing me in. There was nowhere to hide. "I'm walking Forrest over to the pizza place across the street to see if his mom is there."

"*What?* Jenny, hold on. You can't take someone's kid out of the park!"

"I'm taking him to his mother."

"That's what all kidnappers say!"

"Well, I'm sorry, baby, but I can't stay here. Forrest!" I called out, hanging up on Jason for the second time.

Then, out of nowhere, I heard my name. Whipping around, I saw Crystal heckling me and sticking her tongue through the chain-link fence. She shifted an industrial-size Victoria's Secret shopping bag to her other hand and pointed toward a bench near the drinking fountain.

"That's where we did it!" She moved her eyebrows up and down excitedly.

I motioned for her to get her ass inside the playground so we could talk.

"What's going on? It's fucking hot in here." Crystal put on her sunglasses and surveyed the scene.

"I know, right? It's sweltering."

"No. I mean hot as in hot dads." Crystal turned her body toward a heroin junkie by the basketball court. "I'd totally take his morning-after pill."

"I don't think he's someone's dad . . ."

The junkie looked at us, then pulled out his iPhone 6 and made a call. I explained the situation to Crystal, who was too distracted to listen.

"That's Forrest." I pointed over to the boy, who was now charging other children a toll to use the slide. "Can you just watch him while I go hunt down his mom?"

"*What?* That's Sid's playdate? He's an adult. How old is the mom?"

"OUR age!" I said, reminding Crystal that contrary to her Raya profile, she was no longer twenty-one.

Before I could get away, Jason appeared, drenched in sweat and out of breath. Giving up on Crystal, I handed Sid to Jason. "Oh, thank God!"

"Is she back yet?" Jason looked around for Ombré.

"I should have asked for that guy's number," Crystal huffed under her breath, still fixating on iPhone 6.

I proceeded to strip off my purse and leave it with Jason when Forrest came running toward us, screaming,

"MOM!"

Standing behind me was Ombré, looking cool and collected, like she'd spent the last hour taking a nap in a massage chair. She licked pizza sauce off her hands and sipped on an almost empty soda.

"Hey, sorry. Longest line and then they didn't have peppers and so then I went down the block and that place was just as packed . . . Was Forrest okay for you?" Ombré rubbed Forrest's head innocently. "Were you good?"

Forrest batted his eyes and nodded, knowing I didn't have the balls to bust him.

"You guys hungry? I got extra." Ombré waved the piping-hot box of pizza in front of us like it wasn't a hundred degrees out and a slice of pizza didn't contain thirty-five grams of carbs.

"I think we better get going," I said, not even bothering to introduce Crystal.

"Yeah, Sid is done." Jason strapped Sid back in his stroller.

"Oy, stroller naps. Sorry about that." Ombré sighed, surreptitiously sizing up Crystal.

"Actually, it's tricky, but I can usually do a transfer to his crib once we get home," Jason said.

"Really?" Ombré was impressed.

Jason extended the canopy over Sid's stroller, shielding him from the sunlight, then turned to me and explained their conversation as if they'd been having it in Latin. "If I leave him in his stroller to sleep, he'll only do a thirty-minute nap and be a disaster the rest of the day. Gotta get him in the crib to log at least an hour."

"Yaas," I agreed with too much enthusiasm. Crystal looked at me, confused, like I'd just said I loved football.

"I don't have kids." Crystal flipped her hair, smug.

Jason wrapped his arm around me as he opened the gate to leave. Crystal took one more look around, then followed.

I waved goodbye to Ombré and lied that I'd call her again soon.

We walked Crystal to the subway stop, two feet away. She didn't notice because she was already on her phone, contemplating a flirty text to a Dad Bod she met at work. I didn't bother throwing a fit because there was no point. Crystal was who she'd always been. And just because I'd changed, it was unfair of me to expect her to. I didn't need Crystal to be my mom friend, nor did I need Ombré, or No Boobs, or even Dad Bod's wife. I just needed a confidante, someone to talk to, someone I could relate to, and someone who knew more about children than I did. My ideal mom friend didn't need to own Chloé boots I could borrow or know how to give me the perfect cat eye. It took me a minute to see it, but the greatest mom friend I'd ever have had been with me all along.

Jason kissed me tenderly on the cheek as I looked down at Sid, brushing the hair from his eyes.

"Be honest," I said. "Is this the hottest threesome you've ever had?"

8

SOME BODIES THAT I USED TO KNOW

I. DEATH IN VENICE BEACH

I was asleep in my bed, my body still throbbing from being cut in half like a magician's assistant days prior, when suddenly the entire room started shaking. The framed painting above my head swung back and forth on the wall; the unread baby books on my nightstand came crashing down beside me.

"Oh my God! We're having an earthquake! Save the dogs!" I screamed.

I dug through my sheets and scooped up Gina and Teets, hoping Harry was already dead under a fallen dresser.

"Jenny! We have a fucking baby!" Jason sprang from the bed and charged downstairs to check on Sid. By the time I flipped on the lights and stumbled after him, the series of mild tremors had passed. As had my days of giving a shit about my dogs.

Having a dog and then having a baby is like falling in love with someone new while still living with your ex. No matter how hard you try to convince the people around you that it isn't weird, *it is*. People told me that things would change when I had my son, that my dogs wouldn't hold the same place in my life. I considered those people animal haters who didn't cry at the movie *Blackfish*. To think that I could ever prioritize some-body over Teets was fucking preposterous. I was twenty-one years old when I got Teets—barely old enough to take care of myself—and yet somehow, together, the two of us survived. He flew with me all over the country, only taking breaks to refuel on Starbucks breakfast sandwiches and cappuccino foam. He walked me down the aisle at my wedding. He was there when I broke up with my long-term boyfriend, Lance (whose wife isn't secure enough to let me control his life still). He was there when I stopped being anorexic and when I started again and when I finally stopped for good. I sobbed into his fur when I didn't get the *One Tree Hill* pilot, when I didn't get the *Mad Men* pilot, when I didn't get the *Suits* pilot, and when I didn't get the waitressing gig at Maggiano's. (They said that my three weeks of experience as a barista at the Coffee Bean made me more hostess material.) Teets and I were partners in crime. I'd been spooning his matted beige dreadlocks my entire adult life. He wasn't a dog to me. He was a classy fucking gentleman in a fur suit. He raised me as much as I raised him. He taught me how to love, or at least taught me how to love someone who never criticizes and offers only unconditional adoration.

After having Sid, as I was being wheeled into postop, I'd weepily confessed to the attending nurses that Teets was on his way to visit me. Jason had insisted that if we were going to smuggle Teets into the hospital to meet Sid, it had to be covert, but in my doped-up state, under the influence of adren-aline, estrogen, and Dilaudid, it slipped my mind. I was sure they would understand where I was coming from. Teets was my other half. He had to be there to take pictures with Sid and sleep in his Isolette. My pupils were more dilated than my uterus ever had been as I rambled on and on about the bond between a woman and her dog. The nurses seemed to think I was delirious and, luckily, didn't take my ramblings seriously.

When Teets arrived as planned, he popped out of my mom's purse the way Sid was supposed to pop out of my vagina. Confused and decked out in the doggy scrubs I'd purchased online weeks earlier, Teets was lifted up onto the bed to meet Sid. Jason rushed to lock the door, as if we'd just pulled out a gram of celebratory heroin. Sid was busy trying to siphon the first drops of creamy, yellowish colostrum out of my nipples when a cold nose touched his squishy head. Startled, he threw his hands up in the air, decking Teets in the face. I pushed Teets away, trying to soothe Sid.

Teets looked up at me, shocked. He cocked his head to the side, taking in my topless body and the tiny naked man sucking my tits. It was the ultimate betrayal. Sure, he'd seen other tiny naked men sucking my tits before, but I'd never let it stop me from scratching his head or braiding his hair while it happened. And Sid wasn't trying to prove anything to Teets or anyone else. His only game plan was to suck my nipple until it literally detached from my body. Then maybe poop.

It had been a long day. My mom was going to take Teets home that night, leaving Sid, Jason, and me at the hospital to recover. I kissed him goodbye, satisfied that we'd been able to share such a special moment, but Teets still felt snubbed. He refused to make eye contact, jumping into my mom's purse and disappearing.

Three months later, in what he claims is a total coincidence, he was diagnosed with nasal cancer.

Jason and I were in New York, about to go live on Sirius with Jenny McCarthy, when the oncologist called me back with the results. Teets had been having trouble breathing out of one nostril for a few weeks, but I assumed it was just seasonal allergies. Apart from his hay fever and a bee sting when he was two, Teets had always been the epitome of health. Just before Sid arrived, we threw a Bark Mitzvah to ring in his thirteenth birthday. The idea of him not living long enough to see his *quinceañera* devastated me. Jason and Jenny held me in the studio as I sobbed. Teets was my best friend. I didn't know myself without him. I wasn't @jennyandteets without him.

Gathering myself, I appraised Jenny McCarthy as she sat back down in her swivel chair, adjusting her microphone. Could she be my new Teets? Touching the back of her long platinum hair with my hand, I whispered the handle @jennyandjenny just to hear how it sounded and instantly burst back into tears. The fact was, there was no replacing Teets. He had been my life when I had no other life.

Teets's death would mark the end of an era—an era when I was reckless and could wear cutoffs that barely covered my ass. I had other obligations now, an ass to cover, a child to raise, but still, it didn't seem right that Teets had to die, or that I should ever have to own a pair of Bermuda shorts. I'd always figured one day, when the time came, Teets and I would fall asleep gracefully on a bed of Egyptian cotton and never wake up. We'd probably be buried in the same tomb, pharaoh-style, eternally resting side by side in matching mummification Spanx. Or maybe we'd be like Sean Connery in *First Knight,* sent to sea on a giant funeral pyre, then torched by a series of flaming arrows. Either way, we would be together. We were never supposed to *not* be together.

I returned to L.A. and turned my focus to my dying sidekick.

"Unless he is a complete outlier, my guess is you have six months," the vet said, brutally honest.

I couldn't swallow, I couldn't breathe, I couldn't even remember what I was craving for lunch. Teets looked at me with a look that said, "Remember the movie *Terms of Endearment?* Well, this is going to be ten times worse." The vet suggested radiation with the caveat that it would just be palliative, but I shook my head, refusing to draw out his death sentence.

"No, I don't want to have him suffer. I won't do that to him. I wouldn't want him to do it to me." My voice shook.

"Well, it's not painful. It's just a laser we zap him with. We put him under light anesthesia and he wakes up having no idea what happened. Just think about it. We aren't in a rush." With that, she took Teets's chart and left the room.

"She said we aren't in any rush except for the fact that we are in a big fucking rush because he's DYING!" I screamed into my Bluetooth as I drove back from Venice Beach to the house to meet up with Jason.

"Baby? Are you driving? You don't sound like you should be driving."

"I probably shouldn't because I CAN'T EVEN SEE OUT OF MY EYES," I cried.

"Jenny! Are you serious?"

"Who cares, Jason! We are all going to die anyway. What's the point of anything?"

Even at my most nihilistic, I knew what the point was: Sid. As hard as it was going to be, I was going to have to let Teets go. I pulled over to the side of the road and waited to calm down. Teets nestled into my arms, happier than I'd seen him since I'd given birth. Maybe he *had* been this happy post-Sid, but if so I hadn't taken it in. I barely noticed when his water bowl was empty. Our relationship had changed. As much as I promised myself I wasn't going to turn into one of those assholes who cast off their dog as soon as they have a kid, that is exactly what I'd done. And as terrible as it was to say: I loved Sid more. I had to hide it from Teets, because it would break his heart. But I knew I was going to lose him. In a strange way, I already had.

We got out of the car and sat in a nearby park. We reminisced about the past: our first apartment together in L.A., our first kiss, our first fight . . . Like all breakups, you don't just lose that person, you also lose the *you* that you were when you were with them. I was nostalgic for the past because the past felt simpler, less painful, less complicated. I mean, it obviously *wasn't*. I was an anorexic, unemployed actress who spent her days driving aimlessly around Los Angeles with a ten-pound poodle for a boyfriend. But with the distance of time, we're able to make even our darkest hours seem romantic. Those days had already been cataloged in an archive in my brain labeled *Carefree times better than the moment I'm currently in.*

After discussing it with Jason at dinner, I decided I had to try the radiation.

"Who cares if it doesn't give him more time, at least he'll be comfortable," I said. Jason watched as I fed Teets a porterhouse steak off my plate at Wolfgang's.

"Really, is this necessary?" Jason looked around, waiting for somebody else to object so he didn't have to.

"I'm feeding him whatever he wants. He's gonna be dead by the end of summer, so until then, he's living it up!" I was loud and indignant, eager for someone to confront me just so I could shame him for insulting a cancer victim.

I did whatever I could to spend time with him. I invested in a double stroller so he could ride alongside Sid on our afternoon walks. Whenever I left the house to do errands, Teets came with. On the rare occasion that I was forced to leave him behind, he'd widen his eyes and I'd start hearing Sarah McLachlan's "Angel. "

Riddled with guilt, it got harder and harder for me to do anything without him. He accompanied me to business meetings, bridal showers, bikini waxings. I even got his blood work done so he'd be able to travel with us to Tahiti in the fall. And if he died before that, well, I figured it would be a great place to spread his ashes.

As I looked more closely, I realized I'd gotten myself into one of those relationships that my husband had always found himself in (before me, obviously), my white knight complex beginning to infringe upon my own happiness. It wasn't that I didn't *want* to be around Teets twenty-four/seven, it was that I had a baby to tend to and Teets was monopolizing too much of my time. I knew I should be focusing my attention on Sid, but I accepted the situation because I also knew it was temporary. Or so I thought.

Several weeks after his radiation treatment, Teets started to change. His breathing was back to normal, as was his appetite. He was running around, humping things, and barking into thin air. My fragile, glassy-eyed ex-boyfriend had turned into a cocky, arrogant, cancer-beating Lance Armstrong. With every day that passed his sense of entitlement grew. He started bossing me around the house, furiously scratching the door to Sid's nursery if I tried to lock him out. I couldn't make a move without him all over me. He wanted to know who I was talking to, where I was going, what I was eating. Then every so often, just to underscore his dominance, he'd lift his leg and empty his bladder all over Sid.

"Yeah, I just don't understand. I thought you said he'd be dead soon," I said to the vet, two days before I was supposed to leave for Tahiti. It had been just over six months and Teets's health hadn't stopped improving. "Not that I'm disappointed or anything . . . It's just, I planned for him to be dead by now, you know?"

As much as I loved Teets, the truth was, I kind of needed him out of the way so I could focus on my new life with Sid. Every time I pulled Sid next to me, Teets found a way to squeeze between us; if Sid left a toy on the floor, Teets would take it outside to bury it in a mass grave he'd dug. Instead of taking Teets to Tahiti, I decided to leave him in L.A. He was no longer on death watch and we needed a few days apart. When I returned, he looked younger and spritelier than ever. The facial hair he'd lost from the radiation was filling back in. He was starting to look like the dog I had ten years ago.

Jason and I couldn't help but resent him for it.

"Can you believe you were basically ready to put this dog down six months ago?" Jason shook his head as we drove home from the sitter. I looked at Teets, who stood on Jason's lap as he drove, his head hanging out the window. "LIVE STRONG, BITCHES," I pictured him bellowing at the top of his doggy lungs as we passed a pack of Rottweilers. For a split second I had a dark fantasy of pushing him out of the car. It was all just too much! The roller coaster of emotion, the tug-of-war between my past and my future, the fact that I still wasn't sad enough to stop eating. Something needed to change.

By February we were back in New York. Teets was still an egomaniac and I was still trying to adjust to a polygamous life-style. He'd breezed past his fourteenth birthday with ease and was about to make it past Sid's first when I reached my limit. The vet had told me months earlier that when he was ready to go, I'd know it.

"Are you by chance ready to go?" I asked him one night before bed.

Teets looked up from a giant bone he was hoarding in his dog bed. "Not even a little bit," his eyes replied.

"I mean, I love him. You know how much I love him, but how long is this going to last?" I was in bed next to Jason and whispering under the sheets. Teets was drinking water in the living room, so I was certain he couldn't hear us. "I just . . . it's February and I always pictured Sid's first birthday having a sort of Circle of Life theme."

"Like what, you would have made our son's birthday double as Teets's funeral? Are you sick?" Jason whispered, too, equally scared of Teets's wrath.

"NO! God, no!" I gasped in horror. "More like his wake. Super-chill. Lots of dancing. Maybe a piñata in his likeness."

Against all odds, Teets and his nasal tumor Lived Strong all the way through to July, when finally he started slowing down again. Sure, in concept I was ready for things to end. After all, I was only one death in the family away from my goal weight. But as eager as I was for a grieving widow body, losing Teets would undoubtedly be the most painful thing to ever happen to me.

By August, his nasal congestion was back and worse than ever. Even at his most sedentary, his breathing sounded like a Jewish guy in a down comforter store. I tried to teach him to sleep with his mouth open like I did, but the vet said it was impossible. He dropped from nine pounds to five, so thin I could count his vertebrae from a foot away. I'd sworn the first time I did the radiation that it would be the only time, but the second I saw him struggling, I was on a plane back to Los Angeles to do a second pass. All the skepticism about cancer-beating miracle drugs went out the window. My apartment became filled with Metacam, Yunnan Baiyao, Proin, Endosorb, metronidazole, turmeric, green tea, stasis breakers, omega-3 fatty acids, Rx Biotics, Clavamox, and a neoplasia support dog food. I would let Teets go peacefully but not painfully.

The day before his second treatment in Los Angeles, he lost all interest in food. Even the Umami burger I'd picked up for him from the Grove lay cold and untouched on the bathroom floor. I didn't think he was strong enough to make it through another round of radiation, but the oncologist insisted his blood work looked good. So in a last-ditch attempt, I went for it.

Teets narrowly escaped cancer the first time around. He'd outlived his prognosis by nearly a year. I was proud of him for fighting as long as he had. And as frustrating as it was at times, I was eternally grateful that he'd gotten to know Sid and that Sid had gotten to know him. Whether or not Sid would remember him, I had photos and videos and silly stories that would be indelibly etched into my memory.

Sitting in the waiting room of the VCA hospital on Sepulveda Boulevard, I started to wonder if maybe Teets had stuck around as long as he had just to make sure things were serious with my new beau. Once he was sure I was going to be okay, maybe he'd be ready to let me go . . .

Not the case. At fourteen and a half now, he's beat cancer twice and has already made it clear that he has no intention of letting me go anywhere. For his *quinceañera* he has requested a life-size piñata of Sid. When RSVPing, please be forewarned that he does read my e-mails.

II. LAST TANGO IN PARIS, OHIO

Harry should have been a one-night stand. The type of dog you watch for the day, then never see again. He wasn't hostile or mean. His personality could actually be quite charming if you caught him at the right moment, and his looks were unrivaled. He was a gorgeous male model of a miniature pinscher who, like all male models, is best enjoyed at a distance, in his underwear on the back of a passing bus. Taking him into your home and trying to domesticate him is only asking for trouble. Harry and I lived together for the better part of eight years not because I wanted to but because I had no choice. Aside from enjoying long walks on the beach and having little to no patience for candlelit dinners, we had nothing in common—besides Jason. Harry had come with my marriage, and as cold of a bitch as I could be, I would have never forced Jason to give him up—until I did.

I met Harry a couple weeks after I met Jason and I could tell right away he was hot but not my type. He had a great body and an adorable face but he had rocks in his head. He was needy, high-strung, mildly homicidal. He couldn't sit still long enough to listen and if left alone would devour underwear, shoes, wallets, and trash. One time he ate an entire bag of fertilizer and vomited shit all over Jason's brand-new carpet. Another time he devoured a giant pot brownie and spent the rest of the night fucking all the cashmere throws. Next to Teets, who was patient, respectful, and could probably qualify for Mensa, Harry was a total himbo with separation anxiety. He never wanted to be left alone. At night he expected you to spread your legs and let him burrow in. If you left him outside the house, he would bark at the top of his lungs until you opened the door. If a piece of food fell on the ground he would turn into a complete savage, willing to take your arm off in order to consume it. If you invited guests over he would suddenly be compelled to shit in the spot most likely to get stepped in. Like an asshole stepson who was either going to end up moving out of state with his mom or stabbing you to death in your sleep, you just had to keep your mouth shut and keep all your valuables hidden. On more than one occasion I asked Jason's ex if she'd be willing to take Harry back, but even Baz knew better than that. In my most desperate hours I probably offered to throw in her beach caftan to help sweeten the deal, but she still wouldn't budge. Harry was a problem child and everyone but Jason could see it.

I always knew that Harry's demise would be of his own making. As many times as I was tempted to lather his body in chicken fat and take him on a leash-free hike through Runyon Canyon, I refrained. Harry was Jason's dog and the burden of breaking up with/murdering him needed to fall on Jason. Though it was annoying and cost me thousands of dollars in obedience school, steam cleaning, and boarding, I refused to be the bad cop. Instead, I mentally checked out, allowing entropy to take hold until Jason saw fit to do something about it.

For most of the first year and a half of Sid's life, Harry was boarded at a place in Sylmar. I never feared that Harry would intentionally harm Sid, more that his reckless behavior would somehow lead to our house burning down. Unlike Teets and Gina, who are basically throw pillows with eyes, Harry needed constant supervision. He was like that emotional guy at your house party who spends his night on the roof threatening to cannonball into the swimming pool. Unless you were willing to devote your entire evening to looking at his sketchbook filled with *Hunger Games* fan art and hearing about the time he tried to kill himself, he was determined to make a scene. In L.A., Jason and I had space for these kinds of antics. At least there, Harry could channel his restless energy into hunting squirrels or digging mass graves with Teets. But in New York, we didn't have the luxury of outdoor space or playrooms filled with enough toys that you wouldn't notice five or six missing. We were living in an apartment with a baby, a nanny, two other dogs, and three Elmos. And if any of those Elmos were to get chewed apart and spit out under a couch, it would affect all of us dramatically.

Still, once we'd committed to the East Coast full-time, Jason insisted that we bring Harry out of boarding to join us.

"He's my dog, Jenny. He can't just stay in L.A. indefinitely."

I wasn't opposed to Harry staying in L.A. indefinitely, actually. But I *was* annoyed that he'd been with our dogsitter long enough that we'd paid for her face-lift. I had a face to worry about, too. And though I'd tried to block Harry out of my mind, he kept sneaking his way back in. Like that annoying guy you accidentally slept with at a holiday party fifteen years ago who's still inviting you to his birthday drinks, he wouldn't let me forget him.

I tried to separate my own feelings from the equation, and the more I thought about it, the more moving Harry to New York seemed like a bad idea not just for us but for him, too. He needed a life that the city couldn't offer. He needed a life I couldn't offer. Before Sid, I had more patience, a higher threshold for chaos. Now I had a toddler who kicked and screamed and had just mastered the art of opening a door. There was nowhere to hide. Even when I was sitting on the toilet Sid would find me and threaten to stab himself in the head with a curling iron. Jason and I needed to be on high alert at all times, like two racquetball players with freshly minted nose jobs.

It was Sunday morning and the clock was ticking. In less

than a week Jason was flying to L.A. He and Harry hadn't seen each other in more than nine months. Though he missed his dog, I could tell that even Jason was daunted by the repercussions his decision would likely yield. While Jason grappled with his conflicting emotions, I did what I do best: surreptitiously surfed Instagram and judged strangers.

I scrolled aimlessly through my feed before stopping on a picture posted by a woman I'd come to know as @Fleamarketfab. Jen, aka Flea, was a designer I'd bought an Icelandic sheep hide off months earlier when I'd decided I was an interior decorator. Jen had the kind of eye for décor that's so good it makes you want to gouge out your own useless eyes with the arm of a Hans Wegner wishbone chair. I loved her page and her home, and never failed to heart any pic she posted of an Africa juju hat casually hanging next to a fiddle-leaf fig. But on this day, she posted something different. It was a candid snapshot of a miniature pinscher dressed as a dragon. I paused for a minute, trying to remember if I'd ever noticed a miniature pinscher on her page. I knew she had a shepherd and some sort of red-headed foxhound, but I'd never seen a minpin. Maybe this was a new addition? Or maybe she'd had him all along and I just had a mental block that prevented me from seeing minpins in general?

I impulsively shot her a text. "Hey, Jen, Do you have a minpin?"

"Yeah . . . Why?" Jen's phone had the option turned on that tells you the exact moment she'd read your text, letting me know she was a way better person than me.

"Do you want another one?" Having never met her, I

decided there was no point in beating around the fiddle-leaf fig tree. For all I knew, she was already living in her own personal minpin hell.

"Whose?" she wrote back instantly.

I looked at Jason across the room. He sat on the floor with Sid, counting how many blueberries they could balance on Teets's catatonic body. Out of the corner of my eye, I saw Gina sprawled out across a recent issue of *T* magazine, staring at her nails and sunbathing on the windowsill. For approximately two minutes, everything in my apartment was calm. I pictured Harry and what his energy would do to the rarely tranquil environment.

"Mine," I wrote back.

I could see that Jen had read my text, but she refrained from answering. As the owner of a miniature pinscher, I understood how someone offering you another could be taken as a total fuck-you. So, taking Jen's nonresponse as all the response I needed, I turned my attention to a post of Lamby Dunham in a leotard.

A few hours later, Jason and I started our "leaving the house routine," which usually took an hour. Sid was standing on the dining room table refusing to put on pants. I tried to coax him down by offering him a chia bar I'd disguised as a piece of candy.

Just then my phone vibrated in my pocket. It was Jen. She told me that she'd talked it over with her husband and that not only was he open to taking Harry, he was giddy at the idea. Was she serious? I know I had offered, but seriously, what kind of person would willingly open their home to a ten-year-old problem child? What was the catch?

Ultimately, it didn't matter *why* Jen was willing to take Harry in. Only that she was. Now I just had one other person to convince.

"How do you know this person?" Jason stared at me skeptically as he finished his coffee and I soothed Sid by pretending to eat his legs.

"I've known her for months. She's the woman I bought that sheepskin from." I was trying to keep things vague.

"And you've met her in person?"

"She has a big house, three other dogs, her kids are grown, just look at these pictures of her place." I pulled up Jen's Instagram feed, showing Jason her *Architectural Digest*–worthy digs, then went to the kitchen to pack up Sid's diaper bag.

Jason perused the pics, impressed. "Where is this?"

"Umm." I paused, pretending to look for a sippy cup.

"You don't know!" He'd caught me.

"I do," I said, defensive.

"Jenny. You've never met this person, have you?"

"Virtually. Yes. Physically? No."

"So this is a total stranger."

"Who has nearly thirty thousand Insta followers. I think she's legit."

"And where does she live?" he asked again, steering me back on track.

I knew, or at least I thought I knew, that Jen lived in Ohio, but I wasn't sure where, exactly. Fully clothed now, Sid climbed up my leg and demanded a horsey ride out the door.

"I think like Cleveland, Lorain, Paris, Cincinnati, Des Moines . . ." I grabbed the house keys as I listed a few cities that sounded plausible, hoping one was right.

"First of all, Des Moines is in Iowa. Second of all, there is no Paris, Ohio."

"Yes, there is." I wasn't sure there was.

"I think you're thinking of Paris, Texas." The only thing Jason loved more than correcting my grammar, my spelling, or my math was correcting my geography.

"Google it," I said, pretty sure there was a Paris in every state. Jason immediately stopped in place and got on his phone.

"You're right. It's a place," he announced, disappointed. "But I doubt that's where she lives."

"WHO CARES? The point is that she's awesome, with a great environment that she's willing to let Harry live in." I opened the front door and as I did, Sid slapped me hard across the mouth. Gina bolted out dragging her leash behind her, and Teets started wheezing as if he were choking on a chicken bone.

"We can't have him come here," I blurted out.

Jason closed his eyes, resigned. "I know," he admitted weakly.

After talking with Jen on the phone and confirming that she was a dog lover who did indeed live in Cleveland, Jason felt better about the decision. Later that night when Sid vomited chia bar all over his crib, he was more convinced than ever.

There was just one catch: He couldn't be the one to hand Harry over. Jason explained that if he were to see Harry face-to-face there would be no way he'd be able to give him up. If I wanted Harry to be with Jen in Ohio, I was going to have to take him there myself.

The following week, Jason and I flew out to Los Angeles for my brother-in-law's fortieth birthday. After a whirlwind forty-eight hours, Jason boarded a flight back to New York while I waited at the hotel for Harry. The plan was relatively simple: His sitter would drop him off. I would spend the night with him in L.A. Then we'd board an early flight to Cleveland, where I'd meet up with Jen. The next morning, after the drop, I'd head back to New York.

My anxiety mounted when I spotted Maxine, Harry's sitter, in the valet area of the hotel unloading a bag of dog food from her truck. Harry's head popped out of the passenger-side window and he started barking. He looked older than I remembered. I couldn't help but wonder if he thought the same about me. His eyes were slightly foggier, his muzzle completely gray.

"Hi, Harry," I said, my stomach twisting into a pretzel.

Maxine turned to me and waved. She pulled Harry out of the truck and gave him a long, drawn-out hug. For as much time as I'd spent with Harry, Maxine had spent even more. Before agreeing to give Harry to Jen, we'd offered him to Maxine, but she refused. She loved Harry, but she was already drowning in dogs and didn't need one more of her own.

"I'm gonna miss him," she said, holding back tears.

I hugged Maxine tight, realizing that this was most likely the end of our relationship as well.

"You know he's gonna freeze his ass off in Ohio," she said, handing me two doggy sweaters and a puffy jacket before eventually getting in her truck and pulling away.

As per usual, Harry seemed oblivious to what was transpiring around him. He dragged me by his leash, not so much as glancing in Maxine's direction as she drove off. When he was finished peeing on all four corners of the hotel, I walked him up to my room. Once we were alone and he was off his leash, he started racing around, smelling everything. I worried he could still smell Jason on my suitcase. What I knew and he couldn't was that he'd most likely never see Jason again. I was sad for Harry and also sad for Jason. This wasn't the way I wanted it to end for them.

Around six, my friend Adele stopped by to take me to dinner. I left a blanket and water out for Harry. Adele whined about what a bitch I was for abandoning her in Los Angeles and now Harry in Ohio. But she of all people knew the extent of Harry's issues. She stopped complaining the second I threatened to leave Harry with her.

An hour and a half and five baskets of pita bread later, Adele and I returned to a hotel room covered in feces. It seemed inconceivable that Harry could have been solely responsible. I imagined him opening the door with his teeth and inviting other dogs (and maybe livestock) into the room to empty the minibar and then their bowels. But it was only Harry. Perched on my pillow next to a half-eaten mint was a tiny, perfectly round truffle of shit. Harry looked up at us innocently as if he'd just woken from a long nap and hadn't the faintest idea where he was.

"Yikes," Adele said, and gasped.

I tried to stay calm, but this wasn't an accident. The entire room was smeared in shit. There was shit on the coffee table, shit on the couch, on the blankets, on the room-service menu, even on the remote controls. This was a message. Harry wasn't going to take his abandonment lying down. But I wasn't changing my course.

At eight the next morning I was at the airport with Harry strapped to my side. He squirmed in his dog carrier as I sneaked him through security and onto the plane. According to Jason, the plane was already at capacity for in-cabin pets, so Harry had to travel covertly. Seated next to me was a retired couple, and I made small talk, trying not to look down whenever I heard a weird hacking coming from underneath the seat in front of me.

The second we touched down in Cleveland, I called Jason, breathing a sigh of relief. "We made it. Gonna get in an Uber and head to my hotel."

"You booked a hotel?"

"Well, yeah. Where else would I be staying?" I smiled at the retired couple, who looked at me, worried I was going to ask if they had a spare room.

"With Jen."

"I've never even met her!" I said, tossing Harry over my shoulder and disembarking from the plane.

"But she has almost thirty thousand Instagram followers." Jason couldn't resist throwing it back at me.

"I feel like anything under a hundred is still dubious."

"And yet you're fine giving her my dog?"

I unzipped Harry's carrier outside the airport and let him pee while I waited for my Uber. "Let's put it this way, the odds of Jen murdering Harry are a lot less than the odds of me murdering him," I said, corralling Harry into the Uber and heading into the city.

Not wasting time, I checked into my downtown hotel and immediately texted Jen, telling her I was ready to meet. Jen wrote back that she was getting in her car and would be there soon. In the meantime, I decided to take a shower and freshen up. Too scared to leave Harry in the bedroom alone,

I locked him in the bathroom with me. The two of us had been together in bathrooms innumerable times. Often instead of taking the dogs to the groomer, I'd wash the three of them while I showered.

Our eyes connected as I disrobed and twisted the knob as far left as it would go. The sound of water beating down on the porcelain tub evoked a nostalgia I couldn't resist. Harry stared at me as I studied his perfectly chiseled chin. I remembered the countless times I wanted to punt him out a window, as well as the other, fewer times I genuinely appreciated his presence. He'd kept me safe when Jason was out of town, never allowed me to sleep through an alarm clock, always encouraged more cardio. He watched me learn how to be a writer and a wife. All the crazy BBQs, the late-night fights, the insane capers—Harry had seen them all (or at least heard them through the door of our guest bedroom). As hard as it sometimes was to see it, I loved Harry. There was a part of me that would miss him. I felt a pang of remorse in my chest as I sized up his football-shaped torso. Maxine had washed him before bringing him back to me so he'd be presentable for Jen, but he still had flakes of dandruff scattered along his back. In what might have been our last moment alone together, I picked him up and, for old times' sake, gave him a proper bath. Warm water cascaded down our bodies, washing away years of frustration. Like someone you know you're about to break up with, nothing he did seemed to bother me the way it had in the past. I'd freed myself of the relationship and could now just enjoy his company without worrying about how to change him.

Jen was shockingly hot for a woman who primarily used Insta-gram to post photos of her furniture. With long legs and auburn hair, she reminded me of a younger, funkier Connie Britton. She was warm and open and not at all murdery. Nosing his way through her purse, looking for treats, Harry already seemed to feel entitled to all of Jen's generosity. The courting continued for another half hour before I broke them apart to take Jen to dinner. Harry gave Jen a quick once-over, then conveyed to me with his eyes that even though he and I were sharing a hotel room, and even though, yes, we'd just showered together, we were in no way exclusive.

I shut him in the bathroom and escorted Jen out.

Over two plates of trout and a bowl of shishito pep-pers, we talked about Harry, our astrological signs, and how #TheBlondeSaladNeedsToStop. Jen was the type of girl I wished I'd met fifteen years earlier when I needed a roommate who wasn't my sister. She was witty, smart, vulnerable, and more than willing to share her ice cream. If I were a dog, I would've been psyched to land with Jen. Hearing her talk, I stopped feeling bad for Harry and started feeling envious. (I made a mental note not to mention Harry's whereabouts to Gina, who would have split the second she learned that Jen's kids were grown and her dogs slept on custom kilim pillows.) After dinner we drove back to the hotel, where I ran up to my room to retrieve Harry. I was scared to invite Jen up for fear that I'd find the room demolished. Luckily, Harry had behaved. When we got outside, Jen was standing in front of her car like a coachman waiting to help Cinderella into her carriage. I took a deep breath, expecting some sort of scene, but Harry jumped into Jen's car without incident. I poked my head in, hoping to at least share a farewell kiss, but Harry wouldn't budge.

Jen looked at me, embarrassed. "He probably just smells the other dogs," she said, hoping to reassure me. But it was no use. Harry's exit was true to form in every way. He left the way every bad boy leaves, with a nod that says "I told you not to fall in love with me." A weight was lifted as I watched them drive off, then turned toward the hotel and my empty room. My ego was slightly bruised, but I felt stronger for having let Harry go.

The next morning, I sat on my plane bound for New York. I texted Jason and told him that everything had gone smoothly and that I'd be home soon. He shot back a quick response begging me to hurry. Apparently, while he was napping Sid decided to take off his diaper and give his penis some air. Now the entire crib was covered in urine and Jason was trying to scrub the remaining scent out of the mattress. Before powering off my phone I unconsciously scrolled through my Insta feed. My fingers landed on a picture of Harry luxuriating on a Danish loveseat next to a warm fire. I quickly took a screen grab of it, then expanded it on my phone to see if I could gather further intel. I wanted Harry to be happy, just not quite as happy as he'd been with me. And most definitely not this fast. In this case, however, eclipsing me wasn't going to be hard. Jen spoiled the shit out of her dogs, and Harry's adorable *punim* had already earned her a thousand more followers. Their relationship was in its honeymoon phase and I needed to be supportive. I reclined in my seat and tried to enjoy a few more moments of freedom before returning home to clean up someone else's bodily functions. Despite my efforts to do the right thing, to manage the mayhem, I still felt like I was drowning. I might have gotten rid of one problem child, but I had an even bigger one waiting for me in New York. The issues I had with Harry, though annoying, paled in comparison to the future I faced with my almost-two-year-old. Harry might have chewed up all my shoes, but I couldn't begin to imagine the damage he could have done with opposable thumbs.

Fuck! Maybe Harry wasn't that bad after all. He never forced me to watch shitty cartoons or get up at 3 a.m. to make him a bottle. He never bit me in the face because I wouldn't let him cross the street without holding my hand. He was excellent in the car, always cleaned his plate, had zero interest in using my iPad. Under my sweater, I reached down and, in an act of defiance, powered my phone back on mid takeoff. I examined the picture of Harry again, feeling envious now. I knew it would be years before my life would be as serene as his new one—before I could bring my Danish furniture out of storage or light a fire without Sid trying to roast Gina like a marshmallow. I wanted to be happy for Harry, but a part of me resisted.

That asshole better invite me to his birthday drinks.

9
AMAZON PRIMED

Hello, American Express? Yes, I'd like to upgrade to the black card. I was told that a black card entitles me to an airlift out of the jungle if, for instance, I were in a life-threatening situation . . . Well, I can't be too sure, but I just ingested a cup of ayahuasca and it's not looking good . . . Yes, I'll hold."

My fingers tingled as I tried to move them at my side. I snapped back into the present moment, realizing I didn't have a phone and that my mouth wasn't moving. I was all but catatonic on a small foam mat in the Peruvian jungle, sandwiched between my friends Chelsea and Denny, as a camera crew circled around our mosquito-netted yurt and a small garden gnome of a man with blackened teeth and greasy skin chanted and spit into the night air. Sickness swirled in my stomach as I tried to sit up and assess the situation. Denny's body dripped with sweat. His chest heaved with anxiety. He was pale and bony and looked like something you'd see wheelbarrowed probably just busy.

e she doesn't have her phone.

d, she just posted a picture to Instagram twenty
tes ago.

e she's getting a Pap smear.

e I said or did something to offend her.

e she's told everybody around her that she

me and to never bring my name up ever again.

f I were Amy Schumer she would have

red.

am I not Amy Schumer?

am I failing at life?

ing to be so awkward when I bump into her

onths from now and she spits in my face.

I guess we'll just be enemies. Everybody has

es. It's perfectly natural. Something I'll just

o live with.

rote back.

e totally good. I don't know what I was

ng, of course we're friends!

her.

d never done anything to hurt me. She was actu-
ny biggest supporters. It was the pandemonium
round her that seemed to throw me off balance.
my mother, I couldn't help but feel like I had to
h the world. Everyone wanted a piece of her—
d me to use her interest in me as a way of judging
worth.

Chelsea asked me to go to Peru, I felt worthy.

around a concentration camp. Chelsea stared at the shaman, dead sober.

"What's the game plan with your teeth?" she asked.

The shaman didn't respond, just puffed on a hand-rolled cigarette and blew smoke into her face. Chelsea glanced over at me, making only the slightest effort not to crack up laughing.

"I don't feel anything. Do you guys?"

Denny's eyes rolled into the back of his head as he jolted up and started heaving into a bucket placed at his feet, clearly feeling *something*.

Fifteen minutes had passed and the murky brown cigarette water I'd been told was "medicine" had taken over. Though I felt the room spinning like I'd eaten one too many Jell-O shots, I was acutely aware of my environment. I could count the wooden beams overhead. I was able to make eye contact with Chelsea's cousin Molly, standing behind the monitor. I was even self-aware enough to wonder if the deep-scoop-neck tank I was wearing was worth the fifty bucks I'd recently paid for it, or if I should return the same one I'd bought in white. Confident I wasn't going to die, but unsure what was next, I closed my eyes and let my mind wander into the darkness.

Six months earlier, my friend Chelsea had e-mailed me, asking if I wanted to join her in the jungles of Peru to drink a hallucinogenic tea that was supposed to bring you spiritual enlightenment. The experience was going to be one of several drug experiments in a documentary that she was starring in for Netflix, called *Chelsea Does* . . . Still high off the adrenaline rush of Morocco, I wrote back with an emphatic yes before even googling the word "ayahuasca." Admittedly, I was seduced by the idea of another great adventure to share with Sid. But it also didn't hurt that the entire thing was going to be filmed and broadcast on Netflix, where everyone I've ever hated would have the opportunity to see me sexily washing my hair under a waterfall. The fact that it was Chelsea also made the invitation hard to turn down. Six months prior to this invite, I'd been on a yacht with her sailing through atolls of French Polynesia on quite possibly the most decadent vacation of my life. Whenever we traveled together it was a nonstop party. My face would ache from laughing, my body would ache from trying out whatever harebrained adventure sport we stumbled into. Just being in her orbit infected you with a spirit of adventure that could inspire a thousand cannonballs off a thousand rocky cliffs.

I'd known Chelsea before her fancy trips, her fanatic fans, her meteoric rise to stardom. We met when I was twenty-six years old and working on a terrible *National Lampoon* movie. At thirty years old, she'd already written her first book and starred in a short-lived television improv show, but for the most part remained relatively unknown.

"You didn't audition for this shit, did you?" she asked one day in the makeup trailer.

"Umm. Yes?" I said, embarrassed.

"Well, just an FYI, this movie sucks and Nicole Eggert is a hot mess and probably gonna be dead soon."

From day one, I felt like she was the older sister I'd never had. Back then I didn't quite know who I was. There was a fear

inside me that I carried in
a trepidation that prevente
ing my mind. Chelsea, on
about who she was and whe
train of conviction, whose
dor would pave the way
voices. She was saying what
we had the balls to say it. It
yet hard to hold on to the
was her life.

Fame is a funny thing. It
it can bring out the worst. /
fame herself but who's bee
When I met Jason, he was a
him or hated him, but in b
whelmed with excitement w
super-Jewish kid they went
said looked just like him. As
responded to him in a certai

With Chelsea, it was diffe
years, the girl who I'd watch
dle of a Vegas mall, the girl
shitty Charles David heels b
Havaianas to our premiere p
For a person like myself, who
it was impossible not to feel
unworthy. When a normal fri
text them seventeen times in
When an über-famous frien
different series of thoughts:

1. She'
2. May
3. Wei
   mir
4. Ma
5. Ma
6. Ma
   hat
7. I be
   ans
8. Wl
9. Wl
10. It's
    six
11. Fi
    en
    ha
12. Sh
13. W
    th
14. I

Chels
ally one
that swi
Just like
share he
which a
my own
So w

Mommy picked me. It took a few weeks of saying it to myself aloud to remember I was, in fact, a mommy myself, and that traipsing off to the Amazon to do a controversial hallucinogen with a friend who once persuaded me to climb up the mast of a 164-foot sailboat without a harness might not be in the best interest of my son. I intentionally failed to mention my plans to my therapist for nearly five months, seeking counsel instead from the Magic 8 Ball in my friend Lisette's office.

"It is decidedly so!" I announced one afternoon. "How can I argue with that?"

Lisette worked at *The Wall Street Journal,* where I'd recently repurposed her cubicle to be my writing headquarters. I'd met Lisette through my friend Joan Arthur, who had threatened to kill Lisette if she didn't help publicize my first book. Lisette didn't have children and was still a bit of a baby herself, but I'd decided that her access to a printer and the fact that she thought I was pretty was enough to base a friendship on.

"Don't you just shit and vomit the whole time?" Lisette asked, skimming an op-ed online.

"Yeah, but I enjoy both those things." I hit Print on a two-hundred-page script.

"Animal! Be honest, if I'd have asked you to go on this trip, would you have said yes?" Lisette said, invoking a pet name she'd given me the first time she watched me devour a container of sushi in the checkout line at Dean & DeLuca.

"Absolutely not."

"So you *are* only doing it because it's Chelsea?"

"And because it's going to be on Netflix. Oh, and I might reach enlightenment."

Lisette's office phone rang. She picked it up and immediately slammed it back down.

"Who was that?" I asked, concerned.

"My dad. We are in a *huge* fight. Don't worry about it." She paused, then turned to me, dead serious. "Listen, I think my Eight Ball might be lying to you."

"Really?"

Lisette tucked her jet-black pixie cut nervously behind her ears, then poked her head out of her cubicle to see if anyone was listening.

"It lied to me two weeks ago about my remodel and now I'm in for another fifty grand. Or, well . . . my dad is." She gave me an ominous look before turning back to her computer to continue working.

Though it sounded shallow, it did mean something to me that the trip was being filmed. It legitimized the whole thing. It legitimized me. After all, I'd be on a TV show, and as any actor knows, the words "TV show" are basically interchangeable with "reason for living." I wasn't trying to prioritize my career over Sid. But I did feel the need to keep it going so that in seventeen years when he moved out and left me, I wouldn't completely fall apart. And more than that, I wanted to remain interesting, to stay worthy of his affection. I wanted Sid to respect me, to see me as successful, and to never feel like he was solely responsible for my happiness. I didn't want his high school years to consist of me creepily lurking around his locker, waiting for soccer practice to let out so we could go get our eyebrows threaded. I didn't want to reach my fifties before I learned how to Snapchat. I'd worked too hard to let it all go.

And I wanted to be an example for him, to show him that when you put your mind to it, you, too, can end up doing drugs on Netflix.

But the longer I thought about Peru, the more conflicted I became. Unlike my trip to Morocco, I couldn't seem to justify the risks I was taking this time. Ayahuasca was a drug, and I was responsible for another human being.

"It's used to treat addiction and eating disorders and all sorts of phobias that I think you have," Jason said, over a bowl of Naomi's albondigas soup. "If you were telling me you were gonna go drop acid at some dude's apartment in the Bronx, I'd say no fucking way, but I gotta say, I'm not freaked out by this."

"Baby! You freak out when I'm at the gym too long. You're fine with me hallucinating in South America?" I couldn't believe how nonchalant he was being. This was not the Jason I was constantly hiding shit from.

"My sobriety has opened my mind to this kind of stuff." He lifted his bowl to his face and slurped down a mouthful of broth.

"Opened your mind? Or do you just want me to do drugs because you can't?" He seemed sincere, but I was still skeptical.

"A little of both," he admitted.

"I think you need to do it. In my country, we believe it will heal your fear," Naomi added. "You have *a lot* of fear."

"Are you guys serious? You both think I *should* do it?" I looked at Sid dragging a turkey meatball across his plate. He beamed at me. I was getting cold feet and yet the most important players in my life were telling me to go for it. "What if I come back a totally different person who doesn't believe in marriage or makeup? What if I stop wearing a bra and just want to practice Kundalini yoga and drink yerba maté all day?" I looked down at Teets to see if I could get a read on what he was thinking, but he was too distracted by Sid's meatball. Gina screened him from Sid's high chair like a power forward.

If I were kidless, this is the type of trip I wouldn't have thought twice about. But overdosing in the jungle now had consequences far greater than Jason becoming a widower or his ex-girlfriend being able to use her real name on Instagram. If something happened, Sid would be motherless, and that idea filled me with the deepest dread I'd ever known. I couldn't bear the thought of him waking up in the middle of the night and not having a mommy to call out to, of never knowing how much I loved him, of one day trying to understand who I was by dissecting a picture of me taking a picture of myself in a bathroom mirror. My parents had always put their own needs first, and I didn't want to be as selfish. This was my chance to take a different path. A path that *didn't* lead to me being incapacitated in a foreign country.

As hard as I tried to rationalize my actions, I couldn't make peace with my heart.

That night, I shot out of bed, my eyes wide, delirious with terror, my stomach clenching into a giant knot, the kind you can't untangle. The kind you have to use kitchen scissors to cut out.

"I'm not going," I whispered to Jason, picking up my phone and composing an e-mail to Chelsea. I hit Send before I could rethink it.

The next morning, I reread my e-mail and realized I sounded like a complete psychopath in the throes of an existential crisis. It was 6 a.m. New York time and Chelsea was in Los Angeles, no doubt fast asleep. I quickly scrolled through Instagram to make sure that was the case. Stressed that I was perhaps the worst mother in the world and that Chelsea was going to read my e-mail to Jennifer Aniston over brunch, I decided it was time to call my therapist. As much as I valued Lisette's 8 Ball, I needed input from someone who wouldn't fuck with me by saying "Reply hazy, try again."

Later that day, while anxiously waiting for my phone session with Chandra, I got a call from Denny. I answered cheerily.

"Hi! Are you so excited about Peru? Because I'm not gonna lie, I'm starting to freak out," I said. "Oh, by the way, have you heard from Chelsea today?" I tried to make it sound casual.

"No. I never hear from her. But I got your texts," he said, referring to the six messages I'd sent him over the last twenty-four hours reading: "R WE GOING 2 DIE?"

I'd known Denny and his wife, Dakota, for six years. They were the kind of couple you tell yourself that you and your partner are going to turn into when you grow up. Denny and Dakota were freethinking loners who liked each other better than they did anyone else around them. They had two sons and a third on the way. Though their parenting style was incredibly hands-on, they remained open and progressive when it came to their adult lives. In my mind their date nights consisted of an indie concert at the Troubadour, dinner at some cash-only hole-in-the-wall in Thai Town, drinks at a Valley strip club, and maybe a little impromptu ink at a tattoo parlor on Vineland. Dry, acerbic, and fashionably bitter, Denny was like Woody

Allen if Woody Allen had moved to Los Angeles and started working in reality television. Not only did I look up to his relationship and how he was able to balance his role as a father with his role being somebody far cooler than me, I also trusted that the skeptic in him would never do something that might get himself killed.

"This is the opportunity of a lifetime," he said with an enthusiasm I didn't know he was capable of. "Dakota is so jealous she can't go. If she wasn't pregnant right now, we'd probably be doing it somewhere in Topanga Canyon."

"People are doing ayahuasca in Topanga Canyon now?"

"Mainly Josh Radnor, but yeah." I could see Denny chomping on a carrot as he chased his younger child around his living room. "I can't fucking believe I'm about to have another one of these," he said, mostly to himself.

"Do you think I'm being an irresponsible parent, though?" I asked, desperate for reassurance.

"This is a Netflix special. Nobody is going to let anything happen to us. Chelsea is even bringing her own medic. And it's herbal. Have you done mushrooms?"

"Yes."

"Well, it's apparently just like that, only a thousand times stronger . . ." Denny trailed off, unsure if he'd made me feel better or worse. "You'd better fucking come. I hate all of Chelsea's other friends."

Hanging up with Denny, I started to realize that I'd sat with the idea of ayahuasca so long that it had mutated in my head. Having read little more than a few BuzzFeed articles and a Wikipedia page, I'd convinced myself that drinking the tea was as self-destructive as freebasing crystal meth. The reality was, ayahuasca hadn't actually killed anyone. Sure, there had been accidents involving human error, but you could find those same kinds of stories about Ambien, alcohol, or making a Vine while driving. Chelsea e-mailed back assuring me that I was overreacting about the drug and that we were going to have an incredible time. She acknowledged my concerns but brushed past them, like a skydiving instructor would to the person already strapped to her back.

When I finally spoke to Chandra, she did a bunch of mind-gamey shit, asking me why I'd withheld information from her and questioning whether or not I trusted our therapeutic relationship. Coming dangerously close to uttering the words "Reply hazy, try again," she eventually cut to the chase—and even Chandra, who never missed an opportunity to tell me I was being an asshole, seemed unfazed.

"I think it's fine. Lots of people do it. Not a big deal. For some people it can feel like seven years' worth of therapy in a matter of five hours," she said, leading me to suspect Josh Radnor might also be her client. "But *you'll* still need therapy," she was quick to add.

I tried to do a bit more research online, but like looking at my checking account at the end of the month, I was too scared to dig deeply. So, after forcing Jason to do a bit of reading for me and talking it through several more times with Chandra, I decided to keep an open mind and consider that maybe this opportunity had come into my life for a reason. I e-mailed Chelsea's cousin Molly, our production coordinator, to confirm that I was on board.

It was 9 p.m. on a Monday and our red-eye to Lima left at eleven. Travelers and ticket agents moved briskly through the brightly lit departure terminal of Tom Bradley International like it was the middle of the workday. I was hungry and yet not. Anxious and yet resolved. An hour earlier, I'd been on a soundstage in Burbank. For the weeks leading up to Peru, I'd landed another ridiculous television show, and I was working in Los Angeles every Sunday through Tuesday. Since I was going to be stuck on the West Coast for at least two days after my return, I persuaded Jason, Sid, and Naomi to come stay with my sister and wait for me in L.A. The trip was going to be six days in total, including travel, and if I was able to switch my flight in Iquitos on the way back, I might even get it down to five. I'd been away from Sid for longer, but the older he got, the more difficult it was to pull away. Not because I missed him—I did, of course—but because of the way I knew I'd be punished upon my return. I could be working late one night and not be able to give him his bottle before bed and the next morning he would look at me and start wailing "Dada! Dada!" like I was a home intruder. Jason agreed to bring Sid to California, but after getting into a screaming match with my sister at my brother-in-law Larry's birthday party, where she accused him of drinking all the personal-sized Pellegrinos, he insisted they stay in a hotel.

I got my ticket and breezed through security. Molly called, directing me toward the lounge, where she and the rest of the crew were eating samosas and drinking wine.

"I can't believe this is happening," I said, wrapping my hands around her waist and shaking her like a doll.

"It's gonna be awesome!" Molly was eight years younger

than me but felt twenty years more mature. I'd been with her in various predicaments and without fail she always exuded calm, confidence, unflappability. "Okay, so Denny said he's waiting at the gate and Chelsea is at the XpresSpa getting a chair massage. We have, like, fifteen more minutes before we're gonna head over if you wanna buy any almonds or birdseed," she said, poking fun at my disordered eating. We walked out of the lounge, past Duty Free, Starbucks, and Kitson, looking for the XpresSpa. When we found her, Chelsea was facedown on a rickety massage stool prominently positioned at the store's front entrance.

"Hi, baby." She looked up and smiled, her short blond hair pulled into a tight bun. Molly gathered Chelsea's scattered belongings while Chelsea paid her tab. "No, Molly, I hate that bag. We have to leave it. I think it threw my neck out." Chelsea reached over to a satchel she'd unpacked during her massage and handed it to a passing manicurist. "Do you want this?" she asked. The young Korean girl looked at her, confused. "I'm throwing it away unless somebody wants it," she said to the room.

"We gotta go!" Molly took the bag from Chelsea and handed it to the manicurist. "Come on," she barked, pushing us toward our gate.

"I think I only brought one pair of underwear," Chelsea announced as we walked briskly toward the gate. What my own insecurities often caused me to lose sight of was that Chelsea hadn't really changed that much. Her Havaianas might have been upgraded to Manolo Blahniks, but she was still the girl getting the chair massage in the middle of the mall.

At the gate we looked around for Denny, who seemed to

have already boarded the plane. We boarded ourselves, and Chelsea reclined in her seat. She started playing with her sleeping mask while I looked for my row. When I got there, Denny was waiting.

"Oh my God! This is happening!" I said, looking for a jovial high five. Denny had his blanket pulled up to his neck and was seemingly unable to form words. "Denny?" I asked, waving my hand in front of his face.

"This was the worst idea I've ever had," he said, closing his eyes and trying to breathe deeply.

"Denny! What the fuck?! You told me this was a great idea. The whole reason I decided to do this was you." I started to freak out as the doors of the plane sealed shut. Denny shook his head back and forth, unable to articulate a response. Chelsea hung over her seat, aiming a rubber band at Denny's head and shooting. "Who am I supposed to talk to? This person?" She looked at the elderly woman sitting next to her, then back at us.

Our plane to Lima lifted off; there was no backing out. Just over eight hours later we were in Peru.

"Hope you don't mind if we mic you guys before you get off the plane," Molly said, motioning for Chloe and Andre, the boom operator and sound engineer, to bring up some lavaliers. Denny turned to me, hungover but increasingly coherent.

"Sorry about whatever I said last night. I ate some crazy edibles on my way to the airport." He rubbed his eyes and looked at me like he was seeing me for the first time.

"Denny! You scared the shit out of me. For a second you had me convinced we'd made a terrible mistake."

"Oh, we have," he said, serious. Chloe taped a mic to my skin and fed a wire down the back of my shirt.

"What? Why are you saying this?" I looked around, worried the crew was hearing all of what was transpiring.

"I shouldn't have left. My wife is about to have a baby. We have two other kids. It was a shitty, selfish thing to do." Suddenly Denny, my quasi–role model, was sounding exactly like me two weeks ago.

"Remember, this is the opportunity of a lifetime?" I said optimistically. I needed to get Denny back on my bandwagon before I lost my balance and fell onto his. "Look, we are here. We have to make the best of this."

The camera crew retrieved our luggage while Denny, Chelsea, and I were escorted through customs and put on another plane. After a short two-hour flight, we arrived in Iquitos, the city known as the gateway to the Amazon. We checked into a modest hotel with barred windows on the far side of town and tried to FaceTime our loved ones while we could, before disappearing into the jungle the next day.

Once the center of the great Amazon rubber boom, the former banana republic, battered and bruised from years of colonialism, was undergoing a face-lift with the growing popularity of drug tourism. The largest city in the world not accessible by road (the only way in or out is by plane or boat), Iquitos was an eclectic hodgepodge of cultures, isolated from the rest of the world. Crumbling colonial mansions shared the sunlight with pastel concrete warehouses and floating barges with palm-thatched roofs. Latin-influenced foods and flavors commingled with the wild, unfamiliar tang of the jungle.

The next morning, Chelsea walked downstairs wearing the same silk shift dress she'd been wearing the last time we'd vacationed together. She'd bought the dress in Spain the previous summer and hadn't worn much of anything else since. I'd seen her in a winter coat in New York, but I'm not convinced she wasn't hiding the dress under a sweater. It came off while we were in Tahiti, of course, but only after she was told she wasn't allowed to scuba dive in it. Here, a year later, the dress was back in full force.

We cut across town on colorful moto-cars down to the Mercado de Belén, a huge outdoor market that offered the predictable hearts of palm, coco leaves, cow innards, and skewered piranhas. There were fruits I'd never seen at Whole Foods and an extensive array of indefinable jungle products said to cure anything from erectile dysfunction to breast cancer. Lower Belén, where most of the vendors lived, was an expansive shantytown floating on the Río Itaya, a tributary of the vast Amazon. Children sold clothing out of storage shacks along the river basin. Everything was embroidered with a serpent, a symbol of life, rebirth, and wisdom.

Everywhere you turned, there was something about ayahuasca. Throughout the ramshackle stalls it was touted not as a drug but as medicine. I was surprised by the kinds of tourists I kept seeing. They were yoga instructors, doctors, mothers and daughters on college graduation trips, many of them there for their second or third time. One woman I spoke with told me that she'd bought a package online that included a day trip to Machu Picchu followed by a three-day ayahuasca ceremony. Nobody seemed scared, only eager for what new insights they might discover about themselves. Though I couldn't help but wonder if the pursuit of self-understanding was any less narcissistic than the pursuit of Netflix stardom, it did calm my nerves knowing that ayahuasca drew such a varied crowd.

The air was muggy and the sky looked hazy and foreboding as we piled into a long wooden riverboat and prepared for a two-hour ride down the Madre de Dios. It took several tries for our single-engine vessel to cooperate, gargling in a mouthful of muddy water, then choking it back up. But finally, after some prodding and pounding, we were on our way. I looked down at my phone with zero service, good for nothing other than scrutinizing the smile lines in my pictures from hours earlier. Chelsea sat on Molly's lap until she was certain no snakes had managed to slither aboard. Denny tried to open a bag of Qancha, a type of large-kernel corn that is toasted with oil in a hot skillet, but he was already too dehydrated and weak. The arduous demands of travel were no match for his fragile hipster body. I was eye level with the water when I noticed a fleshy pink hump breaching in the distance.

"What the fuck, I think I just saw a school of swimming labias," Chelsea screamed.

Our translator Frieda laughed. "Those are pink dolphins." They didn't look like any dolphins I'd ever seen. They looked like lethargic albino sea snakes with prehistoric beaks. Our guide spoke a few words to Frieda, who informed us that we could swim with the dolphins if we so desired. While getting my vaccinations for the trip, I remembered my doctor saying that men shouldn't swim in the Amazon because there was a kind of parasite in the river that liked to swim up urethras.

That was enough to convince me that animals in the wild need to, as much as possible, be left the fuck alone.

When we arrived at our eco-lodge, Frieda and Molly and the rest of the crew heaved cases of camera equipment up several sets of steep wooden stairs. Chelsea and I clung to each other as we hiked up behind them.

"Gorgeous view," she deadpanned, looking out at the stagnant brown water that surrounded us. In my mind I guess I'd always pictured the Amazon to be more glamorous, more Tarzany. I thought it would at least look like the Rainforest Cafe at South Coast Plaza. Where were the adorable lemurs? The howler monkeys? The safari fries?

Frieda led Denny, Chelsea, and me to an open-air hut on stilts looking out over the water.

"The three of you will be in here." She smiled, gesturing toward three twin beds lined up along a thin divider wall, separating our sleeping quarters from a shower stall. Denny looked at me, despondent. Chelsea looked at Denny, trying to decide whether he weighed less than her. I felt like we were the three bears in an Oliver Stone retelling of Goldilocks. Frieda, like everybody I'd met in Peru, was under five feet tall, with dark curly hair and large brown eyes. She seemed like the type of girl you instantly connect with when you first check into rehab but then quickly realize is the exact type of person who is going to peer-pressure you into drinking again. Molly stormed in and doled out three headlamps, informing us that the resort's generator would be turned off at ten and we'd be without power until nine the next morning. The headlamps had two settings. You could use them either as a bright white lamp or as a flashing red disco light.

"I don't get it." I placed the lamp on my head and switched it to the flashing red setting. "So this is to notify people that I'm in distress?"

Molly shrugged.

"Seems a little subtle, no? We don't think screaming would work better?" I looked over at Chelsea, who'd opened her suitcase and pulled out a digital bathroom scale, the glass kind that belongs in your home and the kind that would definitely get confiscated from your luggage by airport security, not because it was dangerous but just because it was fucking perplexing. "Umm . . . Why do you have a scale with you? Did you pack that?" I asked.

"Denny, get on the scale! I need to see if you weigh more than me," Chelsea demanded. Denny trudged across the room like Eeyore and obligingly mounted the scale. "Oh my God! Denny only weighs two pounds more than me!" Chelsea shrieked. "Denny? Be honest, are you eating, or are you too depressed because you left your pregnant wife?"

"I am depressed. But I am eating. There's just not much I can fucking eat. I've been on this ayahuasca-prep diet for a month and I'm withering away. I'm ready to just drink the tea and have a fucking beer."

"Wait, Molly, we're not supposed to be drinking beer prior to doing this?" Chelsea said. "I thought just no hard alcohol." She looked at Molly, then over at me. Molly had sent us a list of things to avoid before our ceremony, which included all alcohol, salt, pork, fried foods, hot spices, peppers, onions, red meat, cured fish, and overly ripened fruit. We were also instructed not to have any kind of sexual stimulation for at least two weeks leading up to the event.

"I think the only part I stuck to was the celibacy portion," I added helpfully.

﹏

After meeting up with the rest of our crew for an excruciating dinner, where Chelsea, Denny, and I were allowed only chicken broth and yucca, the three of us headed back to our room to try to sleep. Our meager beds were covered in small gnats that had died there earlier in the day. Once the air conditioner shut off with the generator, we were left in total darkness, sweating and mocking the entire situation. We tossed and turned and laughed deliriously at things I knew would never be as funny again. I felt like I was at summer camp.

Trying to get comfortable, Chelsea removed articles of clothing until she was wearing nothing but a bra and her headlamp. ("I need it to pee!" she explained.) After discussing our favorite authors, which of Chelsea's friends Denny and I hated, and who on the crew we would fuck if stranded on a desert island, we eventually fell asleep.

Around 4 a.m., the sound of insects and nocturnal creatures partying outside our open-air windows was so loud it woke me. I sat up instinctively, thinking I'd set the volume too high on Sid's sound machine. Looking around the room, I saw Chelsea fast asleep, her headlamp having somehow made its way down to her ankle and flashing our room red like it was the whorehouse from *Beetlejuice*. I laughed to myself, then reached over and shut it off. As I was lying on my back giggling, waiting to lose consciousness, I reflected on the last year and a half. There was no denying that I'd been running—from the responsibility of parenthood, from the pain of being in love. Alone now, I saw the way I'd been completely at Sid's mercy. Emotions I thought I knew had evolved into feelings so electric and explosive that they tore my chest wide open.

For the first time, I entertained the possibility that maybe tomorrow's ceremony would bring me a sense of peace that I'd unconsciously been seeking.

Denny and Chelsea spent the next day floating in the pool and trying not to eat. It was almost dusk when they finally broke down and shared a plate of jungle noodles, hearts of palm drizzled with olive oil and lemon.

"I told you guys you should have eaten something. I've been eating all day." I offered Denny a half-eaten bag of almonds.

"Don't do it, Denny! Everything we eat is going to get vomited back up," Chelsea said, looking at Frieda for confirmation.

"But I'm so weak!" Denny caved and took three nuts.

"Just one hour more," Frieda said empathetically.

After sunset, we changed into comfortable, easy-to-remove clothes and headed up a vividly green hill toward a large wooden yurt high above the lodge. My heart started racing the way it did when I knew I was about to do any kind of drug. Part of me wanted to run away. The other part of me wanted to charge faster up the hill.

"I'm freaking out. I think I'm gonna have diarrhea before

this even starts." I tucked myself under Chelsea's arms and tried to slow my breathing. Molly held a lantern out in front of us as the camera crew filmed our ascent.

When we entered the yurt, the rest of the crew was waiting. A small video village hid in the shadows as Frieda walked me toward the light. The center of the yurt was round and stark, save for three mattresses, three large buckets, and a tiny Peruvian man smoking hand-rolled cigarettes. His resting bitch face seemed to contain a sliver of sadness. He sized us up and down and started singing. The cameras were trained on our faces as we tried to keep calm and not burst out laughing. The shaman first handed each of us a cigarette, then, once we were finished smoking, pulled out a water bottle that looked like it had been scavenged from under the seat of my car. The repurposed Arrowhead bottle was filled with a murky brown liquid that the shaman had cooked earlier that day. First, he walked toward Denny and poured a shot glass worth of liquid into a cup. Denny, clearly the honor roll student in school, respectfully accepted his cup and drank it. Next, the shaman approached me with a similarly filled cup. Looking down at the turbid water, I panicked.

"Um, I feel like this is a lot for me. I'm sort of a lightweight. I don't really drink much," I said to Frieda, who was sitting off to the side. Frieda translated what I'd said to the shaman, who grunted something back. I could already tell he hated me.

"He says that he isn't giving you a lot," Frieda explained.

"This looks like more than you gave Denny," I said.

"It may not look like it, but we weigh less than Denny," Chelsea interjected. Growing impatient, the shaman told

Frieda that I could drink as much as I felt like having. I took one last lucid look around the room before tilting my head back and gulping it (or most of it) down. When it came time for Chelsea to drink, she didn't hesitate for a moment, just slammed the shot like she was at a beach bar in Tulum.

After we'd drunk, the shaman, also under the influence of the drug, continued singing and spitting into the surrounding darkness. None of us felt anything for the first ten minutes. Chelsea and I giggled and whispered while Denny lay on his back and tried to focus. By the fifteen-minute mark, it was clear we'd lost Denny. I looked over at his clammy white body as he fought to keep from throwing up. "Are you feeling anything?" I asked.

"Umm . . . yeah," he confirmed.

"Is it good? What does it feel like?" His body language already told me everything I needed to know.

"I wouldn't mind for it to be over," he said, then leaned over his bucket and heaved.

"Of course this happens to me. I knew I wasn't going to feel anything," Chelsea complained to the camera. "Jenny? Do you feel it?"

"Maybe? I don't know," I said, like a girl who doesn't know if she'd ever had an orgasm.

Minutes later, I knew exactly what I was feeling. The room started to buzz as I dizzily stood and stumbled to the bathroom. Frieda followed, steering me toward a row of toilet stalls, each with nothing more than a curtain separating it from the rest of the room. The second I sat down, liquid exploded out of me, of the kind that sounds more like you're peeing than shitting. Just when I thought it was over, it would start again.

It was joined by vomiting. For the next ten minutes I did nothing more than sit on the toilet, shitting and puking at the same time.

"SHWAAAASHHHWAA SHWASHWA," the shaman exclaimed, walking toward me and spitting at what Frieda told me were evil demons trying to attach themselves to my body, or, more specifically, to my butt. Freida took out a large glass bottle of something called Agua de Florida, a cheap cologne-like water that smelled of camphor, gin, and poverty. She doused me with the tonic like a salesgirl at Dillard's, assuring me that it would help quell my sickness. The shaman then cut in front of Frieda and started beating me over the head with a wand of leaves, shouting and SHWAAAASHHHWAASHWAAA-ing into my hair.

Once he'd stopped, I heard nothing but a zapping sound coming from above. I tried to look up, but I was too nauseated. Then, suddenly, a giant beetle with what looked like a feather Mohawk fell into my lap and onto the floor. Hanging my head over a bucket, I caught a glimpse of the creature again in my peripheral vision. He had at least eight legs and seemed to be waving at me with all of them.

"Okay, I'm officially fucked up," I whispered to Frieda, who sat beside me, holding my hand and offering wet wipes.

Once there was nothing in me left to purge, I weakly walked back to my mattress.

"You okay?" Chelsea asked, still annoyingly sober.

"I'm so fucked, you guys." I looked over at Denny, who seemed to be in the middle of the worst nightmare of his life.

"I don't think Denny's having the best time. He may have been the wrong choice for this trip," Chelsea said, half empathetic, half trying to contain her giggles. She moved over to my mattress and spooned me lovingly.

My mind drifted into space.

First there was just blackness. Then a symbol spun toward me. I realized it was the Four Seasons' symbol. "Whatever you do, never tell anyone you hallucinated the Four Seasons' symbol," I cautioned myself quietly. Next I saw the more classic "unicorn" vision, followed by a series of moving pictures. I was transported back to my father's home at Gainey Ranch, where I'd spent so many days playing in the pool with my sister; our half brother, Brad; and various nannies. I stayed in the vision long enough to make sure none of the nannies molested us, then moved on to the next location. I was scrolling through my life like it was an iTunes music library. With each vision I'd have an accompanying epiphany, things that sound trite to repeat but carried such monumental weight at the time, like "Nothing matters besides the people you love," "Your husband is an incredible man," and "One day I'm gonna cut my hair into a super-chic silver bob."

Cradled in Chelsea's arms, my mind drifted to Sid. I pictured us doing a synchronized ice-dancing routine in which I spun his meaty little body over my shoulders like the tiniest Ukrainian figure skater of all time. We skated hand in hand, doing double axels and flying sit-spins as the Olympic arena leaped to its feet with sobbing applause. Then it was just the two of us—Sid and me. Holding my leg with both hands, he looked at me and, without saying anything, said everything. My chest heaved and I broke into hysterics. Molly came running out to make sure I was okay, as Chelsea rocked me back and forth, trying to help me calm down.

"SHWAAASSHHHWWAAASHWA," the shaman continued.

"Don't be sad, Jenny. Nothing bad is happening," Chelsea and Molly insisted.

The thing was, I wasn't sad. I was overcome. Sid continued to hold my gaze, communicating the simplest message, and yet the thing I most needed to hear.

"He loves me," I wept, like I was a contestant who'd just been proposed to on *The Bachelor*. "He already loves me. Because I'm his mom and I'll always be his mom."

It seemed so obvious that I couldn't believe it hadn't occurred to me sooner. While I was busy trying to curate my image, to scale mountains, slay dragons, and generally do anything to combat my feelings of unworthiness—Sid already saw me as a hero. I was afraid of pain—of feeling it or causing it. But Sid was my pain, because he was my heart, torn from my body, running loose in the world. I'd thought that if I looked hard enough, I'd find a conclusion that would make the fear subside. I desperately wanted to reach a point where I could say, "I was afraid and now I'm not." But what I was slowly coming to understand, what I think all mothers eventually have to accept, was that I'd always be afraid. Because, though I'd spent the majority of my life resisting it, I was now truly open.

To be honest, it didn't feel great. But it felt better than being closed.

I got back to L.A. a few days later, convinced I'd never do drugs again (for at least the next two months). Jason must have recognized something inside me had shifted a little. When we got to the hotel that night and I collapsed into bed, I noticed he used fewer pillows to build the wall that usually separated us while we slept. Maybe he was sensing a newfound—something. Vulnerability? I couldn't say for sure. All I know is that when I described my trip—the yurt, the shaman, the shit-puking, and finally the visions—it felt as though I was letting him into a part of me I'd never let him access. It was as though having Sid was forcing me to love Jason better, harder, and more.

Frankly, it was fucking exhausting.

As I spoke, I could see a knowing smile creep on Jason's lips, like a grandfather in a Werther's Original commercial. He stayed mostly silent until I was done, then took me in his arms. We stayed that way for a long while, longer than I previously would have been able to tolerate, and then even longer than that. Until what was uncomfortable seemed strangely okay.

Finally he spoke.

"So how drug-free do you have to be before we can make another one?"

ACKNOWLEDGMENTS

Writing about someone in a book acknowledgments is kind of like inviting them to your wedding. By the time this book comes out, I'll probably hate a lot of you. But here's a short list of people I currently care about.

Sid, who I am certain will one day do this all better than me. I love you so much it literally makes me wanna throw up. I promise to always listen, to always be there, to give you every piece of me you ask for. I am honored to be your mother. And I can't wait to know the person you become.

Jason, this is all your fault. Thank you for changing my life. You are my best friend and my eternal muse.

My mother, Peggy, who succeeded in doing it better than her mom. I am so grateful to both you and Dad for your ambition, your kindness, and your athletic bods.

Jhoni, I think I might have been waiting my whole life to find a friend and mentor as supportive as you. You make me want to be a better woman to all women. Well, not all. Just the cute ones. Thank you for teaching me how to tell better stories.

Chelsea, you are one of the cute ones! Thank you for your fearlessness, your friendship, and your loyalty.

Yaniv, I couldn't have done this without you and I wouldn't have done this without you. (Unless somebody offered me a shit ton of money.)

Joe Veltre, thank you for making Yaniv pay me more money.

Jami Kandel, thank you for helming the ship.

At Doubleday, Bill Thomas, Todd Doughty, Margo Shickmanter, Emily Mahon.

Other people who matter: Elizabeth Brown, Missy Malkin, Lynn Fimberg, Jennifer Craig, Joanna Colonna, Deborah Feingold, Bradley Irion, Gita Bass, Dan Maurio, Diablo Cody, Molly Burke, Ramon Walls-Gumball, Brian Walls-Gumball, Jen Lancaster, Melody Young, Nick and Amey Zinkin, Ladurée Sotto, FIKA Tribeca, Allyson Ostrowski, Busy Philipps, Dori Zuckerman, Dan Driscoll, Tifawt Belaid, Lauren Tabach Bank, Allison Stoltz, Samantha Mollen, Chiara Biggs, Elvie Buller, and always Gina, Harry, and the incomparable Mr. Teets.

Jenny put Mr. Teets down on March 14, 2016. He ate bacon three hours before. Despite her frustrations in Chapter 8, not a second goes by that she doesn't wish he was still in her arms silently judging her every move.

ABOUT THE AUTHOR

Jenny Mollen is an actress and *New York Times* bestselling author. She was a columnist for *Playboy* Online and the Smoking Jacket and has contributed to *Cosmopolitan, Glamour, New York* magazine, Elle.com, and *Grubstreet*. She has been heralded by the *Huffington Post* as one of the funniest women on both Twitter (@jennyandteets) and Instagram (@jennyandteets2), and named one of Five Twitters to Follow by the *New York Times.*